The Activist Spirit
Toward a Radical Solidarity

Victor Narro

The Activist Spirit – Toward a Radical Solidarity

Copyright © 2022 by Victor Narro

ISBN: 979-8-9850979-1-7

Cover art by Anna Usacheva

Book Design by D. Bass

Published by Hard Ball Press.

Information available at: www.hardballpress.com

Library of Congress Cataloging-in-Publication Data

Narro, Victor

The Activist Spirit

1.Labor Rights (PA) 2. Labor Union. 3. Immigrant Rights 4. Spirituality 5. Social Justice

Dedication

To my labor activist wife Laureen, in deep appreciation for your love and sustenance over the years.

To all the activists who are in the trenches every
day fighting for justice and a better tomorrow. My
deepest gratitude with radical solidarity for you all.

Contents

Introduction

I brought this book into the world because of my love for humanity and my love for our sisters and brothers who have dedicated their lives to the work of social justice, and to making this world a better place. Whether you are a labor activist, immigrant rights activist, housing or education activist, criminal justice activist or an environmental activist, this book is an expression of my deep gratitude for your commitment and your life's work.

As an immigrant rights and labor activist involved in the work for justice for over thirty-five years, I have learned there is a spiritual core within activism from which we can deepen our solidarity with each other, our interconnectedness, our creativity, our compassion and our depth of love for one another. Tapping into this spiritual core to find sustenance and meaning is both instrumental and necessary in the work for justice. For the work for justice is a form of spirituality in and of itself. It is filled with the values attributed to spirituality – love, compassion, empathy for those in need and a lifetime commitment to bring justice into their lives. This book is a call for all of us to integrate that inner spiritual core into our work in order to make the struggle for justice more compassionate, fulfilling, caring, and sustainable for all of us. To be an activist for justice is to love humanity and all of creation.

This book is designed to help you read, reflect, and go inward. Using the Peace Prayer of St. Francis of Assisi, I share my reflections following each passage. I will bring in messages from Francis of Assisi and what he would be saying to us a peace activist. I will also integrate the teachings and wisdom of other past and current spiritual activists

A meditation moment with a poem or passage follows that provides a space for you to write your own thoughts and reflections. In that sense, this book can serve as your spiritual tool. Through this process of putting your reflections down on paper, every book will be uniquely yours. Through this book and your meditations, you can begin shaping a spiritual focus for your activist life that will be unique to you, but can be shared with others if you choose to do so. For many activists already rooted in their own faith and spirituality, this book can offer new perspectives for them to explore and integrate into their daily activist lives. For activists who do not profess a spiritual belief, you will strengthen your faith that ordinary working people can organize and hold power in this secular world and create a society that cares for and values the dignity of everyone – a society that nourishes and honors all people.

Let this be your faith. Let this be your hope. It is a faith-based ideal, and it needs to be nourished and maintained, like any spirituality or faith. This journey inward will deepen your sense of inner peace and mitigate feelings of despair or powerlessness during the difficult times facing us today in the work for justice. Solidarity evolves from the interconnectedness between all of us in social justice work, which is an important and indispensable part of an activist's life. Just as the work for justice is always changing, we must also embrace openness and acceptance of the transformation taking place deep within our hearts, for that is the wellspring of this radical solidarity. May this book guide you in your journey and work for justice.

A Short Introduction of Francis of Assisi

Eight hundred years ago during the Middle Ages, this humble activist for peace transformed his world and renewed the Catholic Church. He accomplished this by simple but revolutionary acts of practicing his faith as it had never been practiced before. Francis was born about 1181 into an affluent family during a period of incredible violence and warfare. Francis dreamed of knighthood, and he fought in battles against other towns and cities.

The Italian city states and towns during that time were filled with daily violence on a large scale. Many historians believe that Francis participated in the killing and slaughter of other soldiers during battle. During Francis' lifetime, the once dominant feudal system was breaking apart, and these cities and towns were engaged in ongoing strife that led to continuing military conflicts.

During his youth, Francis developed a reputation for self-indulgence and playfulness that made him a hero and leader of his town's young people. He watched as his own town of Assisi was wracked by a civil war and a long-running conflict with the nearby town of Perugia. When Francis was 20, the

3

conflict with Perugia erupted into an all-out war. Inspired by patriotism and deep pride, Francis enlisted and went off to battle. He was captured and put in prison for nearly a year.

Two years later, Francis set out for war again, this time as a young knight of a papal army bound for the Crusades. On his way to battle, Francis had a vision that caused him to become weak and profoundly ill. He returned to Assisi, unwilling to take up where he left off. Ill for almost a year, he struggled with dreams and voices telling him to repair the Church that had fallen. These dreams and visions led him to turn his back on his father's wealthy business and the military heroics of his youth.

Instead, Francis chose a radical life of caring for the poor through his acts of love and humility, where he lived among lepers, the homeless and others that society neglected. Francis was a tough and demanding revolutionary voyager of the human spirit who lived his vision. His life (rather than his words) teaches us what it is like to live with spiritual joy in the service of others. Francis lived a spirituality of compassion rooted in humility and simplicity. The way of Francis from the very beginning was the way of peace, love and service. Francis was an extraordinary person whose response to the world of the 13th century gives shape and motivation to our response to the world of the 21st.

Leonardo Boff, a well-known Brazilian theologian and former Franciscan priest, is one of the founders of Liberation Theology. Silenced twice by the Vatican, he continues his liberation theological activism as a lay priest in poor communities, helping people find a vision that encompasses social justice, human spirituality and most recently, ecology. In his famous 1982 work, *Francis of Assisi: A Model for Human Liberation,* Boff examines Francis' ecological consciousness, his nonviolence, his dialogue with other faiths and his vision of a church centered on the poor.[1]

As a "model of gentleness and care," Francis exemplifies for Boff how the spiritual and the social are never separate, but are intimately bound together. Throughout the book, he delves into the richness of Francis of Assisi's life, and finds there a model of gentleness and care, his preferential association with the poor, his liberation through goodness and service to others, his creation of a popular and poor church, and how he confronted challenges. With Francis of Assisi, Boff states that, "we find ourselves faced with a Christian genius of seductive humanity and fascinating gentleness, which causes us to discover what is most true in our humanity. He belongs not only to Christianity but to all humankind."[2]

In our work for justice, we are all interwoven – ourselves, our lives, the communities we represent and what we are striving to accomplish. Just as Francis' level of empathy enabled him to go deep into someone's heart and share the joy and sadness of that person, we, too, must connect through our hearts and let that connection be the driving force that enables us to struggle together, plan together, and win together. This is true solidarity in action. It is the same spiritual force of unconditional love and compassion for one another that Francis had for all of humanity and for all of creation.

Peace Prayer of St. Francis of Assisi Through the Eyes of a Social Justice Activist

Lord, make me an instrument of your Peace.
Where there is hatred let me sow peace;
where there is injury let me sow forgiveness;
where there is doubt let me sow faith;
where there is despair let me give hope;
where there is darkness let me give light;
where there is sadness let me give joy.

O Lord,
grant that I may not try to be comforted but to comfort,
not try to be understood but to understand;
not try to be loved but to love.
Because it is in giving that we receive,
it is in forgiving that we are forgiven,
and it is in dying that we are born to eternal life.

The work for social justice is a calling. We heed that call by becoming instruments of peacemaking and by service to others. "Lord, Make Me an Instrument of Your Peace," commonly known as "The Prayer for Peace" summons us to that calling. It is the most recognized prayer attributed to St. Francis. Jon M. Sweeney, well known scholar of St. Francis of Assisi and author of many books, provides an excellent historical account of this prayer in his new book, *Lord, Make Me an Instrument of Your Peace: The Complete Prayer of St. Francis, St. Clare and other Early Franciscans.*[3]

The Prayer for Peace was not written by St. Francis or derived from his teachings. The author is anonymous and the prayer is a little over a century old, tracing back to 1912 in France. It first appeared in a French-language magazine called *La Clochette* (The litter bell). A Vatican newspaper published a translation in Italian four years later. Soon afterward, it appeared in nearly every language. Despite all the doubts surrounding the prayer's origins, it is easy to see why the words were attributed to Francis. The lasting influence of this prayer is above all due to how it closely reflects the true spirit of Francis of Assisi.[4]

This special prayer has become a source of meditation and reflection for many involved with mindfulness and spiritual practices. In social justice circles, whenever I mention my belief in the examples and teachings of Francis, many respond with *The Prayer for Peace* and how they have embraced its verses and integrated it into their work.

Like Francis of Assisi, this prayer has universal meaning for everyone, regardless of religious or faith beliefs. One of its appeals may be because, as social justice activists, we are instruments of justice in the same way that Francis could have seen himself as an instrument of God's peace. This prayer is a calling to bring peace and justice into the world around us. In the pages that follow, I will use *The Prayer for Peace* as the framework for sharing how spirituality and the work for justice can walk together hand in hand.

Chapter 1

Lord, make me an instrument of your Peace.

The work for social justice is a calling. It is about finding the goodness in yourself and in others as we move forward together towards a society that realizes a higher good – justice, peace, and equality for all. We strive to find peace in ourselves that connects with peace in others, which then brings about peace in our community. This is our interconnectedness. The work for peace can bring healing and joy to ourselves and to others. Those who work for justice make it their lifetime devotion. This is what makes us special as social justice activists.

César Chávez took on a struggle that nobody thought could succeed. Rooted in the religious tradition he had received from his Mexican family, illuminated with the social doctrine of the Catholic Church, inspired by the teachings of Gandhi, St. Francis and Martin Luther King, Jr., and empowered with best practices of community organizing, he provided a spiritual voice to the work for justice. Like Francis of Assisi, César strived daily to live according to the teachings of the Gospel, in addition to those of Gandhi and Martin Luther King, Jr. Much in the same way as Francis of Assisi, Chávez's spirituality was not an escape from the struggles of life, but a deeper insertion into the human struggles between the growers and the unlimited love that he had for farm workers in their fight for justice.[5]

Before César Chávez became a community organizer, and more than a decade before the United Farm Workers was founded, he met Father Donald McDonnell, who came to the impoverished East San Jose barrio where Chávez was living. The barrio was known as Sal Si Puedes ("Get Out If You Can"). Because there was no Catholic church there, no priest, and hundreds of Mexican American families, Fr. Donald felt a calling to serve in that area.

César, a devout Catholic, met Fr. Donald at the local church. Fr. Donald had been working with Mexican Americans and migrant workers. He recognized certain leadership qualities in César and took him under his wing. As a Franciscan, Fr. Donald introduced Chávez to the social justice teachings of the Catholic Church and to works on spirituality and human rights, including the writings of St. Francis of Assisi and Gandhi. He impressed on César the life story of St. Francis, especially Francis' embrace of sacrificing for others.

Influenced by Francis' teachings and activism, César would come to sacrifice his own life for the plight of farm workers. As he became schooled in Fr. Donald's teaching, César's spirituality based on nonviolence, helping those in need, sacrificing for others, respect for others and for one's self, deepened.[6]

The work for justice is not calling for a select few organizers; nor is it about building a legacy. Peacemaking and working for justice are choices that we make in our daily living. You can do it as an artist, poet, teacher, lawyer, artisan, doctor, researcher or local community leader. The work of justice begins inside you, because, as Francis of Assisi once said, "As you proclaim peace [and justice] with your mouth, make sure that greater peace is in your hearts. Let no one be provoked to anger or scandal through you, but may everyone be drawn to peace, kindness, and harmony through your gentleness." [7]

You must first have peace inside you before you can bring peace to the lives of others. Once you have peace inside you, you are able to bring peace and justice to your family, partners, and friends. Your peace will then extend to your community and into the world. Reaching this level of self-awareness requires a commitment to a daily practice, reflection, and patience.

Holding peace in our heart is a challenge because we are consumed by media and calls for action to address all the injustices and attacks on our communities. We are always on autopilot as we turn towards the noisy part of our brain, where habitual thoughts are negative and pessimistic. Holding peace inside becomes a major challenge because of this non-stop consumption of negative overload, and because of our need to respond and act now, without so much as a moment to pause and reflect.

There is a way, however, to cultivate this inner peace. Daily practice of the little things that enable us to act with compassion and a sense of purpose help to ground us. They enable us to pause and quiet our noisy mind, or at least take it off autopilot and bring it kindness. In this way we create awareness in the present moment. We are then able to tap into this inner peace inside us. We become better activists for peace and justice.

The term *leadership* is used in so many different ways that we have no one accepted meaning for the term. We are often swept up by effective rhetoric in the media, at major rallies, at major conferences, etc. After thirty-five years in the work for justice, I still ask myself: "What makes a good leader?"

César Chávez embraced Francis' model of servant leadership. This form of leadership stresses the importance of the role a leader plays as the steward of the resources that a group or community brings together. Servant leadership embraces compassion and humility as overarching principles. It centers on uplifting community members as the core of leadership development.

The message Francis taught was the one he lived. There was no disconnect between his words and deeds, or his public pronouncements and his private life. Witnessing his faith in action helped people to believe.

Francis made believers out of many through his acts. For Francis, the measure of a good sermon wasn't based on the rhetoric. For him, there was no better sermon than "the practice of the virtues."

Francis once said, "It makes no sense to walk somewhere to preach if your walking is not your preaching." For Francis, walking a great distance from town to town to preach the teachings of the Gospel was useless unless you preached during each step along the way through your acts. In every town, to everyone, Francis preached and walked in peace. He did not do so with great eloquence or with exalted human reasoning, but with deep passion. He preached boldly, flattering no one and making no promises. He did not rely on his words, but on the example of his life in action.

He let his walking do his talking.

Clearing
by Martha Postlethwaite[8]

Do not try to save

the whole world

or do anything grandiose.

Instead, create

a clearing

in the dense forest

of your life

and wait there

patiently,

until the song

that is your life

falls into your own cupped hands

and you recognize and greet it.

Only then will you know

how to give yourself

to this world

so worth of rescue.

Your Reflections On Chapter 1:

Chapter 2

Where there is hatred let me sow peace.

Hatred and anger are strong emotions that often tend to overwhelm and dominate us in the work for justice. Hatred and anger can consume and destroy our mental, emotional and physical health. They can lead us to committing unjust and harmful acts. As activists, we must learn to recognize and embrace these feelings of hate and anger and not try to bury them. Rather, we can use our joy and compassion to transform them. This is the nonviolent response to transforming anger and hate.

These daily turbulent emotions can be dominant in the work for justice. Whenever I have a moment of anger, sometimes with a bit of hate creeping in, I take a pause and imagine my anger as a beautiful baby in need of nurturing. I wrap my blanket of joy and compassion around this baby and hold it gently in my arms close to my heart. This visualization helps me to embrace my anger and be kind to it with compassion and understanding.

The historical encounter between Francis of Assisi and the Sultan of Egypt, Malik al-Kamil (Sultan al-Kamil) beautifully illustrates this concept. It is the story of meeting and embracing a stranger or perceived enemy and saying there is a better way than resentment, suspicion and warfare.

The story of this historic encounter, which resurfaced during the 20th century, provides a powerful parable for today, and we must revitalize its significance to let it guide us.[9]

In the political turmoil of the 13th Century "Holy Roman Empire," people were locked in a culture of war as the empire united in a series of Crusades against Muslims, Jews and others labeled as "heretics." The Western portrait of Sultan al-Kamil was skewed by Crusader propaganda and lack of basic knowledge about Muslim society and faith by Christian writers. In Egypt, however, the Sultan was known for his tolerance toward the Christian minority. He was a cultured man who loved learned conversation with scholars in his court. Sultan al-Kamil was rooted in the spiritual belief of peace and compassion. His beliefs eventually led him to broker a peace with the Crusaders by ceding Jerusalem to the Christians in an attempt to save the lives of the people in the city.

The story of the meeting between Francis and Sultan al-Kamil opened a door to respect, trust and peace. Francis followed his prophetic nonviolent resistance to the violence of the Crusades by embarking on a journey to meet with Sultan al-Kamil and bring him his message of peace. He embarked on dangerous journeys three times, but strong storms prevented him from successfully crossing the Mediterranean sea to get to Egypt.

His moment finally arrived during the summer of 1219, in the midst of a Crusade that was killing thousands of people in the sweltering heat on the banks of the Nile. The leaders of the Christian

army warned Francis not to cross the bloody battlefield between the two armies to seek out the
Sultan. Francis did not accept the Pope's call to war.
Instead, he continued on with his goal of meeting
with Sultan al-Kamil and embrace the Muslims,
knowing full well the risk of his undertaking.

Crossing the treacherous battlefield, Francis and
his traveling companion, Friar Illuminato, set foot
on the outskirts of the Muslim camp. The Muslim
soldiers seized them and took these two barefoot
monks dressed in worn out patched brown tunics
to appear before Sultan al-Kamil. No one actually
knows what was said, since Francis did not speak
Arabic and Sultan al-Kamil didn't speak the French-
Italian dialect Francis used. It was their way of being
together, the attitude of mutual respect and understanding, as well as their belief in one God, prayer,
charity, and peace that appealed to both men.

Sultan al-Kamil had his circle of Sufi holy
men with him to help him with translation. When
Francis made it clear he was not there on behalf of
the Pope's army, but as an ambassador of his God,
this intrigued the Sultan even more. When Sultan
al-Kamil saw Francis' enthusiasm and courage, he
listened to him willingly and pressed him to stay
with him. They spent four days together in mutual
respect and understanding.[10]

Francis' desire to share his spirituality and
message of peace with the Sultan, without insult-
ing Islam or refuting Mohammed, was unique and
disarming. During that brief moment in history
when Francis and Sultan al-Kamil were with one

another, their dialogue turned into an embrace of each other as human beings driven by their religious belief for a higher good. According to many accounts, they both shared a meal together. The image of Francis peacefully breaking bread at a banquet with Sultan al-Kamil demonstrates the appreciation that they had for each other and the respect for their differences.

Francis was changed by the experience and came away deeply impressed with Islamic spirituality. His yearning for peace with Islam is especially apparent in his suggestion that his brothers and sisters live quietly among Muslims and "be subject" to them rather than engage in disputes, a provision that appears in an early version of the code of conduct for his order, its Rule. When Francis was ready to leave and return to Italy, Sultan al-Kamil showered him with many gifts and treasures. Because he had no interest in worldly wealth, Francis refused them all, except one special gift: an ivory horn used by the muezzin to call the faithful to prayer. Francis used it to call people to prayer or for preaching.

Francis and Sultan al-Kamil teach us today about compassion and understanding in how we accept one another and embrace our differences. When political beliefs, government institutions and cultural differences divide us, we must seek solidarity with our sisters and brothers, ever mindful that we seek the eventual unity of all people.

While we oppose systems of oppression and the cultures that support them, we bear no hatred for the unwitting followers of that culture. Rather, we invite and entreat them to give up their life of cruelty and arrogance and to embrace a life of tolerance and equality.

Francis and Sultan al-Kamil engaged in active listening with their hearts, which enabled them to speak through compassion and loving speech, and not anger, frustration or fear. Really listening, and hearing without judgment, is a gift that we can give to one another to enhance all of our lives. Francis and Sultan al-Kamil teach us that when we are really heard and the other understands our meaning and emotions, we feel valued and respected. There is no more precious gift to give or receive than to listen to the words of another. This process of active listening and loving speech enable us to be mindful of and respect the dignity within every one of us.

If unchecked, feelings of anger and hate create a violent response. They become a strong stimulus and our response is to fight and respond in kind, or to avoid the situation and then allow it to consume us and make it worse. In 2005, the National Science Foundation published an article regarding research about human thoughts per day. The average person has from 12,000 to 60,000 thoughts per day. Of those, 80% are negative and 95% are exactly the same repetitive thoughts as the day before.[11]

I am reminded by the well-known psychologist and holocaust survivor Viktor Frankl when he said, "Between a stimulus and a response, there is a space. It is within that space that you find your growth and development."

Our minds are often on autopilot, consumed with all these negative thoughts coming in and out. At the same time, the average person breathes in around 17,000 breaths every day. Beathing is life medicine. The relationship between the breath and spirituality is ancient. Breathing can become our antidote to feelings of anger and hate. Creating focus and awareness of our breathing can help us pause, quiet our noisy mind filled with so many thoughts, and embrace our anger with self-kindness. We then are able to look at it from a non-judgmental perspective. The outcome will be a response grounded in understanding and compassion.

The Guest House
by Jelaluddin Rumi[12]

This being human is a guest house.
Every morning a new arrival.

A joy, a depression, a meanness,
some momentary awareness comes
As an unexpected visitor.

Welcome and entertain them all!
Even if they're a crowd of sorrows,
who violently sweep your house
empty of its furniture,
still treat each guest honorably.
He may be clearing you out
for some new delight.

The dark thought, the shame, the malice,
meet them at the door laughing and invite
them in.

Be grateful for whoever comes,
because each has been sent
as a guide from beyond.

Your Reflections on Chapter 2:

Chapter 3

Where there is injury let me sow forgiveness.

Francis of Assisi best exemplified the lifelong journey of striving towards a state of unconditional love and unconditional forgiveness. This is a state of being that most, if not all of us, will be unable to achieve in our lifetime. The important learning here is to uphold these two attributes as goals we aspire towards in our work for justice. These two principles are at the fundamental core of the spirituality of nonviolence. They are what made Francis a genuine non-violent activist for change in society and within the Catholic Church 800 years ago.

The act of forgiveness is a very difficult one for many of us. It is especially difficult for those who grew up in the United States, where individualism and severe, destructive, self-criticism are perceived as core values needed for a successful and profitable life. These forms of self-criticism are based in shame and guilt. A forgiving heart, however, is a necessary value for activists to implement every day if we are to have meaningful change in the work for justice.

When you forgive someone, you are not forgetting or excusing the act that caused you or another harm or injustice. You are not pardoning or condoning the act. To forgive is an act of courage. You decide to no longer hold anger or bitterness towards that person. It is an emotional release and an act of liberation, because you are no longer bound by the anger that the person caused you to hold. Anger and bitterness towards a person can lead to personal hate, which can destroy your mind, body, and spirit.

Nor does forgiving someone mean that you have to engage with that person. Often, it may be unwise to do so. It simply means that you no longer hold the person in your negative thoughts filled with anger and bitterness. It is your healing moment for bringing justice to yourself. A forgiving heart is an important part of the work for justice.

Francis had a very complicated relationship with his wealthy father, Pietro di Bernardone, a cloth merchant who made a fortune in the mercantile economy during the Middle Ages. Pietro refused to honor Francis' calling to a life of peacemaking and poverty through the teachings of the Gospel. He would go in search of his son, determined to return him to his former life. When word reached his father that Francis was the center and target of commotion in the streets, he immediately went to find his son, not to rescue him, but to destroy him. He was like a wolf pursuing a sheep. When Pietro found Francis, he dragged him home in shame and disgrace. He kept him locked in a room for days, determined to recover the worldly-wise child he had known and understood. At first, he used words, then came physical blows, and finally chains. But rather than being broken, Francis was instead strengthened and made more certain of his new purpose in life.[13]

One day Francis came across San Damiano, a tiny chapel on the plain below Assisi. He stepped into the chapel, perhaps to seek comfort on a hot day, or perhaps to pray. The ornate, Byzantine style life-size crucifix over the alter seemed to speak to him, "Francis, go and repair my house, which has fallen into ruin." Francis thought that God was speaking of the little church in which he prayed. Ever the man of action, he acted on God's order.

After his epiphany at the church of San Damiano, Francis experienced another defining moment in his life. In order to raise money to rebuild this little church, he sold a pile of clothing from his father's shop, along with his horse. His father became furious upon learning of his son's actions and subsequently dragged Francis before the local magistrate and local bishop, accusing him of theft.

The bishop told Francis to return his father's money, to which his reaction was extraordinary: he stripped off his clothes, and along with them, returned the money back to his father. This was Francis' big moment, when he decided once and for all to abandon his worldly ties and to instead embrace the call of God. The event is credited as Francis' final conversion, and there is no indication that Francis and his father ever spoke again. While Francis and Pietro never engaged in a process of reconciliation, Francis never made any statements indicating that he held on to any bitterness or anger towards his father.

Felicia Sanders survived Dylann Roof's shooting rampage on June 17, 2015, that killed nine Black parishioners who had gathered at the Charleston,

South Carolina, church for Bible study. She was there when her son, Tywanza Sanders, was shot to death. During an emotional sentencing hearing, Sanders told Roof, "I forgive you." She went on to say, "That's the easiest thing I had to do. But you don't want to help somebody who don't want to help themselves. May God have mercy on your soul." Felicia Sanders represents how to transform anger into compassion during the process of forgiveness.[14]

In *The Book of Joy: Lasting Happiness in a Changing World*, His Holiness the Dalai Lama and Archbishop Desmond Tutu teach us why we need joyfulness during our times of struggle and adversity. The occasion for their book was the Dalai Lama's 80th birthday. It inspired these two close friends to get together in Dharamsala for a full week of talk about something important to them. The subject was joy. Both the Dalai Lama and Archbishop Tutu have been tested by great personal and national adversity, and they shared their personal stories of struggle and renewal. Now that they are both in their eighties, they especially wanted to spread the core message that to have joy yourself, you must bring joy to others.[15]

> "Joy is the reward, really, of seeking to give joy to others. When you show compassion, when you show caring, when you show love to others, do things for others, in a wonderful way you have a deep joy that you can get in no other way."[16]

During their week together, the Dalai Lama and Archbishop Tutu had a dialogue about forgiveness as freeing ourselves from the past. As the Archbishop said, "No one is incapable of forgiving and no one is unforgivable." During this discussion, the Dalai Lama continued, "Forgiveness does not mean we forget. You should remember the negative things, but because there is a possibility to develop hatred, we mustn't allow ourselves to be led in that direction – we choose forgiveness."

The Archbishop was also clear about this when he talked about forgiveness. For him, forgiveness does not mean you forget what someone has done, contrary to the saying "forgive and forget." Not reacting with negativity or giving in to the negative emotions does not mean you do not respond to the acts or that you allow yourself to be harmed again.

Forgiveness does not mean you do not seek justice or that the perpetrator is not punished. To this the Dalai Lama added that the power of forgiveness lies in not losing sight of the humanity of the person while responding to the wrong with clarity and firmness. To which the Archbishop added, "Forgiveness is the only way to heal ourselves and to be free from the past." [17]

As Jack Kornfield says, "Forgiveness is giving up all hope of a better past." The past is done, it does not help to go back to it over and over, wishing an event had been different. In that sense, forgiveness is really not about someone's harmful behavior; it's about our own relationship with our past. When we begin the work of forgiveness, it is primarily a practice for ourselves.[18]

Does this mean that we should not be feeling anger about all the atrocities committed by a government and condoned by cultural norms, such as the ones that occurred during the Trump administration? Absolutely not. Feelings of anger are normal for many of us who work for justice. What matters more is how we channel those feelings of anger. With the right perspective and awareness, we are able to transform feelings of personal anger towards someone like Trump into what Archbishop Tutu refers to as "righteous anger." During his decades in the struggle against the apartheid government of South Africa, he was able to transform personal anger into righteous anger against the acts of injustice.[19]

Righteous anger is an important ingredient of joyfulness in the work for justice. Throughout the country, many activists—young and old—are coming together to engage in dialogue and collective strategies on creating a sustainable movement to fight back for the long haul.

Through his teachings Francis of Assisi reminds us about the unforgiving spirit: It blocks the flow of grace and mercy into our lives, causing us to live in a stagnant state of regrets, animosities and grudges. Forgiveness simply means releasing those who have offended you from your own hostility and anger. It is the freedom of no longer holding anguish or bitterness inside you. It does not change the act that caused you harm or pain, nor does it prevent you from denouncing injustice. Forgiveness creates room in your heart for love and mercy, which are necessary for bringing peace in the world.

Prayer Before the Prayer
by Desmond Tutu and Mpho Tutu[20]

I want to be willing to forgive

But I dare not ask for the will to forgive

In case you give it to me

And I am not yet ready

I am not yet ready for my heart to soften

I am not yet ready to be vulnerable again

Not yet ready to see that there is humanity in my tormentor's eyes

Or that the one who hurt me may also have cried

I am not yet ready for the journey

I am not yet interested in the path

I am at the prayer before the prayer of forgiveness

Grant me the will to want to forgive

Grant it to me not yet but soon

Can I even form the words?

Forgive me?

Dare I even look?

Do I dare to see the hurt I have caused?

I can glimpse all the shattered pieces of that fragile thing

That soul trying to rise on the broken wings of hope

But only out of the corner of my eye

I am afraid of it

And if I am afraid to see

How can I not be afraid to say

Forgive me?

Is there a place where we can meet?

You and me

The place in the middle

Where we straddle the lines

Where you are right

And I am right too

And both of us are wrong and wronged

Can we meet there?

And look for the place where the path begins

The path that ends when we forgive.

Your Reflections On Chapter 3:

Chapter 4

Where there is doubt let me sow faith.

Brother David Stendil-Rast is a Benedictine monk who has been a spiritual interfaith world leader for over 60 years. Brother David founded the art of gratefulness in daily living. In his book, *Gratefulness, The Heart of Prayer: An Approach to Life in Fullness,*[21] he explains how it is not happiness that makes us grateful. It is gratefulness that makes us happy. Every moment is a gift. There is no certainty that you will have another moment, with all the opportunity that it contains. The gift within every gift is the opportunity it offers us. Most often it is the opportunity to enjoy it, but sometimes a difficult gift is given to us and that can be an opportunity to rise to the challenge.[22]

For Brother David, grateful living calls us to actively engage with faith and courageous trust in life. He teaches us that we sit with faith when we enter stillness, when we are in awe, and when we act with love. Brother David believes there is something greater than our current circumstances that we can imagine, and we make ourselves willing to surrender to, rather than control, life in these times. Once we commit to this path, we begin to deepen our exploration of faith, because we recognize its nourishment and the many gifts it has to offer us.[23]

Poet Rabindranath Tagore beautifully said, "Faith is the bird that feels the light when the dawn is still dark." Faith allows us to be this morning bird where we sing at simply the prospect of a new morning.[24]

Brother David writes about gratitude as an important part of the work in creating a more just society. In order to create a better world, we must have faith in each other.[25] This is how radical solidarity comes into our lives and our community. This is how people of all beliefs, backgrounds and perspectives unite in the cause of justice.

In one of his talks, *Revolutionizing the Revolution*,[26] Brother David discusses many of the great founders of spiritual traditions who have initiated a revolution. He believes we need a revolution, but many of the revolutions that we know operated within the old domination system. When those who had been oppressed took power, they continued many of the oppressive methods of the previous rulers.[27]

Brother David argues that this is what many revolutions have done throughout history. He suggests that what is needed is a revolution that revolutionizes the very concept of revolution. He talks about how the Buddha did it, and how Jesus Christ and others did it.

A revolution that takes down an oppressive system and replaces it with a new one can only succeed when there is a revolution inside of us. There must be an inner transformation in our sense of community, compassion and love for one another. The true revolution must not be imposed by force or violence. It must be a nonviolent commitment to justice for all.[28]

From the Christian tradition he refers to this as "the third way." When there is aggression and the domination system is perpetuated, ruling by force and the threat of violence, there are two normal ways to respond: flight or fight. Flight, or just giving in, is the way many people act. Fighting back is the traditional revolution. The third way is non-violence. That was Jesus' way: turning the other cheek.

Turning the other cheek is not giving in. Turning the other cheek was profoundly revolutionary. For Brother David, revolutionizing the revolution is about having faith in a nonviolent response to oppression. Nonviolent actions turn the system of oppression upside down and defeat it in a supreme act of faith. Activists can fiercely oppose an oppressive system, but ultimately, the system that you build must be founded in compassion and love.[29]

Faith is a vast concept which, in our lives and in the world, expresses itself in myriad ways. Whether we have something we would call a faith tradition or if we believe we have no religious faith in a traditional sense, we all live informed by some degree of faith in what we cannot see, cannot reason, and cannot know. Faith can be trusting in life, trusting in your inner core or wisdom to guide you in the present situation, whatever or wherever it may be. For social justice activists who are secular in their beliefs, your faith may be in the ultimate goodness of humanity, or in the ability of working people to unite in the struggle for a more just world.

For many activists, their notion of faith may be the "justice" that Dr. Martin Luther King, Jr.

referred to in his famous quote: "The arc of the moral universe is long, but it bends toward justice."[30] Brother David refers to faith as "courageous trust," and believes that gratefulness is at the heart of this experience.[31] This definition of faith can pertain to trusting in life itself, or in the source that holds all of life. Regardless, the definition of faith that informs our work for justice holds an essential respect for all religious and spiritual traditions, and is a wide, inclusive embrace for all their expressions. Deepening our faith means expanding our hearts and what we can hold.[32]

"Faith" can be the noun with "trust" as the verb to put it into action. We trust life and ourselves to put faith into action. We trust in a higher good or an ideal to put faith into action. We are then able to see justice as a path towards this higher good. "Trust" tells us this higher good is real and based on what we experience daily in our work.

To accomplish the work for justice, we have to trust ourselves and one another as activists. This can be a challenging process for many of us. We must work to dismantle judgmental self-criticism and self-doubt in ourselves and towards others. By self-criticism and self-doubt, I am referring to the "inner-critic" inside of us that shows up and absorbs us during times of uncertainty or difficulty in our work. We all have an inner critic — an inner voice that expresses criticism, frustration or disapproval about our actions. It might sound like, "You should," "Why didn't you?" "What's wrong with you?" or "Why can't you get it together?" The actual self-talk is different for each of us, as is its frequency or intensity.

A cultural norm deeply entrenched in this country is the belief that harsh criticism or guilt-induced comments will motivate behavior. Perhaps the thinking is that if you realize that your actions are not good enough or ideal, you will want to change. The "inner critic" sets a limitation on ourselves and on what we believe is possible.

Others in our lives may make "helpful," yet critical comments to reinforce and control our behavior or control their feelings. We also use judgmental or controlling thoughts within ourselves as a way of coping with fear, shame, and the unknown. Over time, these comments (within ourselves and from others) internalize and become our "inner critic," the persistent negative self-talk that leads to despair.

When we are self-critical and doubt ourselves, we cause injustice to ourselves. Self-doubt and judgmental self-criticism prevent us from being our true selves and fully present in the work for justice. Instead of allowing our "inner critic" to absorb us, we should see every activity as a learning experience. Engaging in the learning process helps us to dismantle our "inner critic," bring kindness to ourselves, and broaden our horizon to realize greater potential as activists.

Francis had to trust the voices inside him telling him to seek a new life rooted in the teachings of the Gospel. He trusted his "inner voice" to choose this path and to guide him. All the scrutiny, ridicule and verbal attacks that he experienced from his friends, parents and townspeople caused him to trust himself and this new journey even more. In the same way, we must trust that we aspire to a higher good, and the work for justice is the path to it. We must bring ourselves fully in the daily work by embracing the failures, setbacks, and challenges. We must trust and embrace this journey.

The Journey
  by Mary Oliver[33]

> One day you finally knew
> what you had to do, and began,
> though the voices around you
> kept shouting
> their bad advice–
> though the whole house
> began to tremble
> and you felt the old tug
> at your ankles.
> "Mend my life!"
> each voice cried.
> But you didn't stop.
> You knew what you had to do,
> though the wind pried
> with its stiff fingers
> at the very foundations,
> though their melancholy
> was terrible.
> It was already late
> enough, and a wild night,
> and the road full of fallen
> branches and stones.
> But little by little,

as you left their voices behind,
the stars began to burn
through the sheets of clouds,
and there was a new voice
which you slowly
recognized as your own,
that kept you company
as you strode deeper and deeper
into the world,
determined to do
the only thing you could do–
determined to save
the only life you could save.

Your Reflections On Chapter 4:

Chapter 5

Where there is despair let me give hope.

Krista Tippett, host of the On Being Project, the popular independent nonprofit public life and media initiative, focuses on hope in her New York Times bestseller, *Becoming Wise: An Inquiry into the Mystery and Art of Living*.[34] She refers to hope as a calling for those of us who can hold it for the sake of the world. For Tippett, hope is distinct from optimism or idealism. It has nothing to do with wishing for good outcomes. Instead, hope "references reality at every turn and reveres truth." For Tippett, hope "lives open-eyed and wholehearted with the darkness that is woven ineluctably into the light of life and sometimes seems to overcome it." [35]

Hope, then, is a choice that becomes a practice to develop a renewable resource for moving through life as it is, not as we wish it to be. Through hope, wisdom emerges precisely in those moments when we have to hold seemingly opposing realities in a creative tension and interplay: power and frailty, birth and death, pain and hope, beauty and brokenness, mystery and conviction, calm and fierceness, mine and yours.[36]

But hope also calls us to attend to the world that is waiting to be born. When we encounter ugliness, betrayal and destruction, hope turns up as bravery, creativity and unfathomable dignity. We then see beautiful lives everywhere, stitching new relationships across rupture, seizing new life out of loss.[37]

In the work for justice, hope can nurture an awareness of the reality of a situation that is having an impact on a community. Hope helps activists bring empathy and compassion into a situation where someone or some group is suffering. We need empathy in our work, and lots of it. Hope enables us to stand in the darkness with and not run away from those in deeply hurt communities. It enables us to connect our hearts with the suffering of others – much like how Francis developed empathy for the lepers and homeless of his time period.

Empathy and compassion lead us to interconnectedness, which then creates more hope. Francis lived deeply in empathy and compassion. He knew they were the roots that nourish our interconnectedness with one another – our heart-to-heart connection. Empathy is our heart reaching out to the heart of someone in despair and sharing in the suffering with them. It is being wholly present – mind, heart, and soul – with someone who is suffering. Compassion then springs forth as we act to address and relieve the suffering. This is the hope of activism in action at its deepest level, much in the way of Francis of Assisi.

Interconnectedness therefore becomes an important and indispensable part of the work for justice. Francis would spend long hours with each member of his first group of followers. He lived the heart-to-heart connections with them. Similarly, in the movement for social change, we are all interwoven – ourselves and our lives. This becomes the collective interwoven web of trust, the deep relationships, and the responsibility to one another. This is our interdependence in our work – the value of trusting in hope that we are doing what is right in the struggle for justice.

Thich Nhat Hanh, a world-renowned Vietnamese Buddhist Zen Master, poet, scholar, and human rights activist, is considered the father of "Mindfulness." He influenced Dr. Martin Luther King, Jr. to become actively involved in the opposition to the Vietnam War. Dr. King nominated him for the Nobel Peace Prize in 1966. In his Fourth Mindfulness Training relating to joy and hope, Thich Nhat Hanh shares the following:

> Aware of the suffering caused by unmindful speech and the inability to listen to others, I am committed to cultivating loving speech and compassionate listening in order to relieve suffering and to promote reconciliation and peace in myself and among other people, ethnic and religious groups, and nations. Knowing that words can create happiness or suffering, I am committed to speaking truthfully using words that inspire confidence, joy, and hope. When anger is manifesting in me, I am determined not to speak. I will practice mindful breathing and walking in order to recognize and to look deeply into my anger. I know that the roots of anger can be found in my wrong perceptions and lack of understanding of the suffering

in myself and in the other person. I will speak and listen in a way that can help myself and the other person to transform suffering and see the way out of difficult situations. I am determined not to spread news that I do not know to be certain and not to utter words that can cause division or discord. I will practice Right Diligence to nourish my capacity for understanding, love, joy, and inclusiveness, and gradually transform anger, violence, and fear that lie deep in my consciousness.[38]

As Francis did with his group of followers, we as activists should create our own sense of community that becomes our "inner core," a spiritual incubator that helps us grow, develop and serve. For Francis, the way to a fulfilling life was in the service of others. Francis was ready to give of himself to live in compassion towards others.

We have the freedom to choose healing and love as a way of life. For Francis, spiritual growth leads directly to service. It is incomplete if it focuses only on what it does for you alone. Spirituality that does not reach out beyond ourselves is like a body without hands. Love that is not communicated through demonstrable acts is love unexpressed. Thich Nhat Hanh says, "If while we practice, we are not aware that the world is suffering, that children are dying of hunger, that social injustice is going on everywhere, we are not practicing mindfulness. We are just trying to escape." [39]

There can be a feeling of emptiness that creeps in when the work of activism becomes a routine of daily activities and tasks. Much of our daily work in the movement is about the fragility of life, dealing with so many lives in the balance, and not knowing what's going on or what will happen next. But in the end relying on our inner strength to believe that the need to love and be loved is inherent in everyone who we help. This helps us realize that it is the relationships within our daily work that should become the central focus. There is really no meaning in a task or activity unless there is a deep inter-connection with our spirituality, our "inner core," and with one another in our work for justice. Francis said, "No matter who you come across in your daily living, either friend or foe, even thief or robber, you should receive all with kindness,"[40] and that "love is more powerful than knowledge or judgment." [41]

Allow
by *Danna Faulds*[42]

> There is no controlling life.
> Try corralling a lightning bolt,
> containing a tornado. Dam a
> stream and it will create a new
> channel. Resist, and the tide
> will sweep you off your feet.
> Allow, and grace will carry
> you to higher ground. The only
> safety lies in letting it all in –
> the wild and the weak; fear,
> fantasies, failures and success.
> When loss rips off the doors of
> the heart, or sadness veils your
> vision with despair, practice
> becomes simply bearing the truth.
> In the choice to let go of your
> known way of being, the whole
> world is revealed to your new eyes.

Your Reflections On Chapter 5:

Chapter 6

Where there is darkness let me give light.

Francis and his followers found their depth of empathy, compassion, joy and love in the midst of their own suffering and when healing others. They experienced deep joy when they could carry out the teachings of the Gospel in a radical way of daily living by serving the poor, lepers, homeless and sick, and they challenged the corruption in the Catholic Church and government institutions.

Much in the same way, we as activists have the capacity to share deep empathy for others. Choosing to live a life of serving others, as activists we have in our inner core a deep level of empathy to tap into when addressing the needs and suffering of others. We become a wellspring of compassion.

You can never fully put yourself in the situation of another who is suffering. Instead, you strive to center yourself so you are able to look at that person's situation from their eyes and their perspective. Your activist deeds become a shining light for those who suffer in their time of darkness. Together with other activists, you combine all your shining lights into a powerful force that can overcome any darkness. A popular quote attributed to St. Francis states, "All the darkness in the world cannot extinguish the single flame of a candle."

Long-time civil rights activist and public

theologian Ruby Sales has been a shining light for me. Born in Jemison, Alabama, on July 8, 1948, Sales suffered many hardships during the civil rights movement but was not discouraged. After earning her B.A. in American history in 1971 from Manhattanville College, where she was a National Council of Churches Merit Scholar, Sales enrolled in graduate school at Princeton University.

Sales taught adult education in Boston for a year, and then worked as director of the Citizens' Complaint Center in Washington, D.C. From 1986 to 1988, she taught courses on the civil rights movement and African American women's history at the University of Maryland before becoming affiliated with the National Women's Studies Association. She served as director from 1989 to 1991 of Black Women's Voices and Images, an initiative to wed research to action on issues affecting Black women. For the following three years she worked as director of Women of All Colors, coordinating a broad coalition of progressive organizations to work on issues affecting all women.

In 1994, Sales entered the Episcopal Divinity School in Cambridge, Massachusetts. She studied feminist, African American and liberation theologies with an emphasis on race, class and gender issues, and in 1998 received her Master of Divinity degree.[43] Her training as a seminarian prepared her to launch SpiritHouse in 2000, a nonprofit organization focused on community organizing and spiritually based community building.[44]

While studying at the Tuskegee Institute in Alabama, Sales became involved with the state's Freedom Summer voter registration drive. One afternoon on August 20, 1965, as she and Jonathan Daniels, a young white seminarian, stood in line at a corner store, a man shot and killed Daniels for standing behind Sales in line. Unnerved and unable to speak significantly for seven months, Sales determined to attend the trial of Daniels' murderer, Tom Coleman, and to testify on behalf of her slain colleague.[45]

Sales' spiritual activism, or public theology, connects her Black spiritual roots, founded in Black folk religion with a philosophy of nonviolence. Instead of a retaliatory religion, African American folk religion is predicated on right relations, love and nonviolence. For Sales, the role of spiritual activism in the 21st century will be a redefinition of community and our relationship to each other. She believes it will be a challenging, but also an exciting moment in activist theology, because it could expand our understanding, as well as the reality of a global Beloved Community. For Ruby Sales, activist theologies must have hindsight, insight, and foresight. This is complete sight, and it says that it's not an "I" sight, it's a "we" sight.[46] Sales carries with her this whole notion of right relations. This is the cornerstone of how she imagines justice.

Sales points out that love is not antithetical to anger or being outraged. There are two kinds of anger. There is redemptive anger, and there is non-redemptive anger. Redemptive anger is the anger that moves one to transformation and human up-building. Non-redemptive anger is the anger that white supremacy roots itself in. It is important to make this distinction, because people think that anger, in itself, is a bad emotion. For her, it depends on where you begin your conversation.

Sales became involved in the Southern Freedom Movement not merely because she was angry about injustice, but because she loved the idea of justice. That is where she begins her conversation.

Most people begin their conversation with "I hate this," but they talk less frequently about what it is they love. Here is where Sales' teachings became a shining light in my work. She believes that we have to develop a conversation that incorporates a vision of love along with a vision of outrage. She does not see them as being over and against each other. You must actually see and embrace them both; you can't talk about injustice without talking about suffering. But for Sales, the reason why she wants to have justice is because she loves everybody in her heart. And if she didn't have that feeling, that sense, then there would be no struggle.[47]

Ruby Sales explores a fundamental question of what it means to be human. She points out that we live in a very diverse world, and to talk about what it means to be human is to talk with the simultaneous tongue of universality and particularities. For Sales, we must wrap our consciousness around a world where people bring vastly different histories and experiences, but at the same time, a world where we experience grief and love in some of the same ways. The question to consider is, how do we develop theologies that weave together the "I" with the "we" and the "we" with the "I"?[48]

Today, we often witness white supremacist and other hate groups that feed on love for a select few while expressing contempt and derision for others whom they deem inferior and unworthy. Francis would say such an expression of love for a select group that allows hatred for others is not really love at all. It is hate disguised as love. For him, love is unconditional, without any qualification or selection. The story of St. Francis and the Three Robbers highlights this teaching.[49]

One day, three murderous thieves showed up at the friars' hermitage of Monte Casale, which was midway between Assisi and Laverna. They asked for some food to eat, but the guardian refused. Instead, he reproved them harshly for their crimes and their depraved way of life and sent them away. Francis returned to the hermitage a short time later with a sack of bread and a jug of wine that he had just begged for. Upon discovering what the guardian had done, he became very upset. Francis reprimanded the guardian and ordered him to go out in search of the thieves with the bread and wine he had just procured. The guardian was to ask them for their forgiveness for his cruelty. Then he was to implore them to change their ways and commit no more criminal acts. If they would promise these things, Francis would provide for all their needs.

When the guardian caught up to the thieves, he did as Francis instructed. They were taken aback as they took the food and wine from him and ate. Listening to his humble words, the thieves started to feel sorrow for the dissolute lives they had led. Their hearts began to be converted.

The thieves decided to go back to Francis and ask if their crimes were too much for God's mercy.

Francis assured them that the mercy and good-ness of God are infinite. They changed their ways and became friars. The desire that Francis had for these three thieves to experience God's mercy was the same desire he had for all people to know God's forgiveness.[50] This desire led to the establishment of the Perdono (the Pardon) of Assisi that is cele-brated every year.

Francis had the capacity to go deep into some-one's heart and share the joy and sadness of that person. As social justice activists, we have the potential to connect through our hearts and let that connection be the driving force that enables us to struggle together, to fight together, and to win together. In reaching such a potential of human relationship, we nourish the spiritual core that enables us to move forward with deep collectivism. This is true solidarity in action in the social justice movement – our interconnectedness and the spir-itual force of love and compassion for one another, much in the same way of the unconditional love that Francis had for all of creation.

I Am the Light
by India.Arie[51]

I am light, I am light

I am not the things my family did

I am not the voices in my head

I am not the pieces of the brokenness
inside

I am light

I'm not the mistakes that I have made

Or any of the things that caused me pain

I am not the pieces of the dreams I left
behind

I am light, I am light

I am not the colour of my eyes

I am not the skin on the outside

I am not my age

I am not my race, my soul inside is all light

All light, yeah

I am divinity defined

I am the god on the inside

I am a star

A piece of it all

I am light

Your Reflections On Chapter 6:

Chapter 7

Where there is sadness let me give joy.

The work for justice today has never been more challenging and taxing for those of us who labor daily in the trenches. At the same time, it has been inspiring to see that our resilience and resistance have not waned, but are growing in many ways, from local community and neighborhood projects to massive mobilizations. One important way to continue sustaining this work is through joyfulness. By joyfulness, I am not talking about comparing our situation with others who are suffering, which is looking at circumstances from our self-centeredness. Instead, it is about being joyful that today's injustice, crisis and adversity provide us with the opportunity to apply ourselves, our talents and gifts as activists to win justice for those in need.

Francis acquired his spiritual joy through acts of simplicity with love and compassion towards others during their time of need and suffering. For Francis, it was important for his followers to embrace joy daily through both the good and the challenging times. No matter what the day brings, the fact that we have a day to live in our purpose as activists is a reason to have joy in our hearts. Let us embrace the joyfulness.

Francis had a special affection for the joyful. So important to him for a true spiritual life was joy of spirit that he made it part of his rule for his followers: "Do not go about with a gloomy countenance or a hypocritical sadness. Rather let the world see your joy in the Spirit. Show everyone the fruits of the Spirit, good cheer and generosity."[52]

For Francis, spiritual joy relied on his interconnectedness with others. We are all interconnected with one another through our hearts. We connect through our joy and through our suffering. This sense of interconnectedness is essential for us to achieve our highest fulfillment in our work. When we work together, we must prioritize uplifting one another in joyfulness, especially during the long struggles. We must connect with one another to have a shared joy and be in community. The interconnectedness of our loving and caring for one another must be inherent in our work.

We find joy in the work for justice through, and with each other. When we are part of campaigns to fight injustices and improve the lives of others, the joy that we all experience in our victories should connect with the spiritual joy inside each one of us. It must be a shared and deep joy, the connectedness of our loving and caring for one another. From a standpoint of organizing, this may be seen as the highest level of solidarity. In a way, this presence of sharing one another's joy and suffering becomes a form of radical solidarity within and among ourselves. It is the power of this shared, collective joy that sustains us as activists as we fight together for justice.

Throughout *The Book of Joy*, the Dalai Lama refers to emergent scientific research showing how we are most joyful when we focus on others, not simply on ourselves. Bringing joy to others is the fastest way to experience joy oneself. It also becomes a way to address fatigue and burn out, which lead to a breakdown of our mind and body. According to the Dalai Lama, even ten minutes mindfully considering the well-being of others can help one to feel joyful for the whole day. When we close our hearts, we cannot be joyful. When we have the courage to live with an open heart, we are able to feel our pain and the pain of others, but we are also able to experience greater joy. The bigger and warmer our hearts, the stronger our sense of aliveness and resilience. This being of joyfulness is indispensable when we find ourselves trying to achieve a strong measure of sustainability during a crisis, such as the coronavirus pandemic.[53]

Generosity of the spirit is the truest expression of spiritual development. It takes time to develop. Give the world your love, your service, your healing, but also your joy. We should imagine ourselves as an oasis of peace, a pool of serenity that ripples out to all of those around us. Doing so enables us to be less self-centered, less self-regarding, and more self-forgetful. Compassion and generosity are at the center of our humanity. They make our lives joyful and meaningful. As Martin Luther King, Jr. once said, "We must learn to live together as sisters and brothers, or we will perish together as fools."[54]

Thich Nhat Hanh teaches us that when we think we are "doing something wrong," we are somehow "failing at happiness." Being able to enjoy happiness does not require that we have zero suffering.

In fact, the art of happiness is also the art of suffering well. When we learn to acknowledge, embrace, and understand our own suffering, we suffer less. Not only that, we are also able to go further and transform our suffering into understanding, compassion, and joy for ourselves and for others.[55]

With her powerful teachings, bestselling books, and retreats attended by thousands, Pema Chödrön is one of the most popular American-born teachers of Buddhism. She teaches us the tonglen practice as a method for connecting with suffering—ours and that which is all around us—everywhere we go. It is a method for overcoming fear of suffering and for dissolving the tightness of our heart. Primarily it is a method for awakening the compassion that is inherent in all of us, no matter what life is bringing you at that moment.

Tonglen practice, also known as "taking and sending," reverses our usual logic of avoiding suffering and seeking pleasure. In tonglen practice, we visualize taking in the pain of others with every in-breath and sending out whatever will benefit them on the out-breath. In the process, we become liberated from age-old patterns of selfishness. We begin to feel love for both ourselves and others; we begin to take care of ourselves and others. Tonglen can be done for those who are ill, those who are dying or have just died, or for those who are in pain of any kind. It can be done either as a formal meditation practice or right in the moment. For example, if you are out walking and you see someone in pain—right on the spot you can hold on to loving thoughts for that person in your mind and heart. You can begin to breathe in their pain and send them healing energy.[56]

According to Chödrön, you can practice tonglen for all people, for everyone who wishes to be compassionate, for everyone who wishes to be brave. If you are doing tonglen for someone you love, extend it out to all those who are in the same situation. If you are doing tonglen for someone you see on television or on the street, do it for all the others in the same boat.[57] Finally, Chödrön teaches us that compassion is not "a relationship between the healer and the wounded. It's a relationship between equals. Only when we know our own darkness well can we be present with the darkness of others. Compassion becomes real when we recognize our shared humanity."[58]

One of the most difficult things for us to accept is that there is no realm where there is only happiness and no suffering. This does not mean that we should despair. Suffering can still be transformed. As soon as we open our mouth to say "suffering," we know that the opposite of suffering is there as well. Where there is suffering, there can be happiness. If we focus exclusively on pursuing happiness, we may regard suffering as something to be ignored or resisted. We think of it as something that gets in the way of happiness. If we know how to embrace our suffering and the suffering of others, we can transform it and suffer less ourselves. Knowing how to suffer well is essential to realizing true joy, especially in the work for justice.

Coping
by Audre Lorde[59]

It has rained for five days
running

the world is
a round puddle
of sunless water
where small islands
are only beginning
to cope
a young boy
in my garden
is bailing out water
from his flower patch
when I ask him why
he tells me
young seeds that have not seen sun
forget
and drown easily.

Your Reflections On Chapter 6:

Chapter 7

O Lord, grant that I may not try to be comforted but to comfort.

As activists, we are agents for peace. We are love and compassion. In providing love and compassion to those in need, we are providing love and compassion to ourselves. From the perspective of the activist work for justice, Francis teaches us about the "false self" or ego-centered self.

Francis the peace activist teaches us that simplicity is needed to control the ego. For him, simplicity is a way to guard yourself from engaging in ego-centric actions, and where instead you act from a genuine place of the heart. It can be a constant struggle, as we often seek affirmation and praise from others. But to act from a place of love and connection rather than for recognition makes for a simpler, freer life. If we can never give up our ego-centric attitude completely, we can still act out of empathy and love for others.

Simplicity lies in where we place our hearts and how we shift from our ego-centered self to our core-self where we can connect with our compassion and goodness. It is from this core-self that we are able to serve and help others from a place of genuine love, and not from one of self-centeredness disguised as compassion.

Simplicity becomes the soil in our spiritual garden from which our values grow and develop. This virtue of simplicity enables us to see our work as less of an emphasis on individualism and self-gratification, but instead we focus the awareness of our actions more on connecting with the lives of those in need and caring for their well-being. Once we are able to make this shift, we find this sense of simplicity that enables us to help others from a place of genuine love and compassion, and not from one of self-centeredness.

By practicing this virtue of simplicity, I come nearer to my acts becoming more genuine and coming from a place of goodness in my heart, and not my ego-centered self. To simplify my life as an activist lies not so much in what I rid myself of as in what I do to focus on my giving and sharing. This does not mean, however, that we must never engage in self-praise for our work as activists. We need to regularly praise ourselves and others for making the choice to live a life of working for justice. We should praise ourselves for our daily work to better the lives of others and bring about a more just and humane world. By doing so, we are not claiming to be special or great, but only that we are using our time to serve and bring comfort to others with deep gratitude. This is an act of self-kindness in our work for justice, not an act of egoism.

Dorothy Day was connected with poverty her entire life. She first encountered poverty in the slums of Chicago, where she lived as a teenager. She later saw it all around her in New York City, where she moved after dropping out of college and lived for more than six decades. Even before the Great Depression, Day had been sensitive to the plight of the poor, a sensitivity that ultimately shaped her calling. The writings of Upton Sinclair helped form Day's interest in the labor movement and deepen her awareness of the struggle between economic classes. At thirty, she converted to Catholicism. In the years that followed, she started a radical newspaper and began opening what she called "houses of hospitality" for those who needed something to eat and somewhere to stay.

The Catholic Worker Movement would serve the poor in more than two hundred communities. Under Day's guidance, it would also develop a political agenda, taking prophetic stands against racial segregation, nuclear warfare, the draft, and armed conflict around the world.

Although ailing in health during her later years, Day continued to champion justice. Her pilgrimages during this time led her to Rome to receive Communion from Pope Paul VI, to India to meet Mother Teresa and speak with novice nuns about nonviolent protest, and finally to California where she was jailed in her final protest, supporting the United Farm Workers with Cesar Chavez.[60]

By the time she died, in 1980, Day had become one of the most prominent thinkers of the left and doers of the right. In her lifetime, it was the secularists who called Day a saint. The Catholic Worker Movement still exists, with nearly two hundred houses of hospitality around the world. Its newspaper, the *Catholic Worker,* is still published and sold for a penny, and it still promotes the revolutions of the heart. Dorothy Day's influence is still felt in the Democratic Socialists of America.[61]

For Dorothy Day, our greatest challenge is "how to bring about a revolution of the heart, a revolution which has to start with each one of us." She demands patience and a deep awareness of the small tasks that are required to accomplish justice. She reminds us to "lay one brick at a time, take one step at a time." While we may not live to see the fruits of our labor, "our work is to sow; another generation will be reaping the harvest." Day teaches us that if we have faith in what we are doing, protesting and fighting against injustice, then we are indeed casting our seeds, and there lies the promise of the harvest to come.[62]

Archbishop Hélder Câmara was an early and important figure in the movement that came to be known as liberation theology in the late 1970s. He served as Archbishop from 1964 to 1985, during the military regime in Brazil. He did social and political work for the poor and for Human Rights and democracy during this period of military rule. Câmara preached for a church closer to the poor and the excluded community members, and he advocated for nonviolence. He is quoted as having said, "When I give food to the poor, they call me a saint. When I ask why they are poor, they call me a communist." Similarly, Francis identified with the poor and marginalized groups, and participated in their struggle for survival, always working for their liberation. He was also cognizant of their plight to being scorned and rejected by other classes. In connecting Câmara with Francis, Leonardo Boff states the following about fighting for the working poor: "One can appreciate the truth of Archbishop Hélder Câmara, the great realizer of Saint Francis in our midst: 'No one is so poor that they cannot give, nor so rich that they cannot receive.' In the giving and the receiving, one is nourished and builds human life as human, beyond class differences. In the giving and receiving, the poor feel that their own poverty is humanized. In this context, courtesy, 'sister of charity and one of God's qualities,' availability, humble service, and the profound gentleness and compassion of Francis with the most needy all require relevance. They are forms of communication that humanize and liberate."[63]

Câmara is saying that the poor and the humble can teach us and transform us. The church and all community organizations seeking to end oppression need to be engaged in a transformative process of servant leadership where they can be transformed by the poor and community members impacted by the injustices they are addressing. It is in this relationship of giving and receiving where we can work together with community members to address the root causes of injustices and poverty, and transform ourselves in the process.

For Francis, simplicity was fighting for equality in a world of savage disparity through the teachings of the Gospel. The world of Francis, much like ours today, was one where the mercantile trade system was dominating and taking over the traditional church-run economy of the Middle Ages. Like the global economy of today, this transition to a new economic model during Francis' time created deep social inequalities and disparity of wealth. Much like today's struggle for economic justice, Francis and his followers focused on improving the lives of the poor, sick and homeless victimized by the injustices of this mercantile economy.

Hope of Loving
by Meister Eckhart[64]

What keeps us alive, what allows us to
endure?

I think it is the hope of loving,

or being loved.

I heard a fable once about the sun going on
a journey

to find its source, and how the moon wept

without her lover's

warm gaze.

We weep when light does not reach our
hearts. We wither

like fields if someone close

does not rain their

kindness

upon

us.

Your Reflections On Chapter 7:

Chapter 8

Do not try to be understood,
but to understand.

When we act through and from a deep well of compassion, we are able to live and experience each other's joy, happiness, suffering and difficulties. Compassion begins with a connection that is genuine and heart-to-heart. As activists, we are always engaging with one another and with those in need. The question becomes whether we are "fully present" for one another. This requires that we engage in deep listening with our hearts. Do we really listen to one another, or do we talk past one another? Are we listening with our hearts, or are we just hearing what we want to believe in furtherance of our position or narrative?

The work for justice requires that we engage in daily active and deep listening with our heart, which will then enable us to speak through compassion or loving speech, especially during moments of anger, frustration, or fear. Really listening without judgment is a gift that we can give to each other to enhance our lives. When we are really heard, and the other person understands our meaning and emotions, we feel valued and respected – a condition necessary for happiness. Engaging in active listening requires daily practice. We are always prone to being judgmental and always looking at situations from a place of self-centeredness where we hide within our self-protective shield. Active listening means that we are truly embracing the humanity of the person in front of us. Active listening is not formulating a response in our minds at the very same moment that someone is expressing their feelings. Active listening enables us to look at a situation from different angles and perspectives. It is fully taking in and embracing the other person without formulating judgment.

There is no more precious a gift than to listen deeply to the words and comprehend the feeling of another. This process of active listening and loving speech will enable us to be mindful of and respect the dignity within each of us. Thich Nhat Hanh teaches us, "The most precious gift we can offer others is our presence. When our mindfulness embraces those we love, they will bloom like flowers."[65] Sometimes, being fully present in deep listening and embracing is all we can do. Some situations may never be "fixed," but can only be fertilized, watered, and given the sunshine of our mindful presence. It is when we drop all our clinging to self-concerns and offer our naked, vulnerable humanity to another person. It is this profound connection with another person that forms the soil upon which positive growth and change takes place. It is this deep connection that brings the deep bonds of solidarity in the work for justice.

The story of St. Francis and the Wolf of Gubbio is one that has been told and retold throughout the ages. The variety and breadth of the re-telling and reimaging speaks to the universality and appeal of the story. One day, a large lone wolf began to appear around the town of Gubbio, terrifying in physical size and ferocious with rabid hunger. This wolf not only destroyed other animals, but many of the citizens believed that he captured and devoured many of the children. This wolf kept all the citizens in such danger and terror that when they went outside the town, they went armed and guarded as if they were heading into a deadly battle. The mayor of the town sent for Francis, having heard that Francis had a special way of connecting and communicating with animals. When word reached Francis about this wolf, he immediately set out to the town of Gubbio.[66]

As soon as Francis entered the city, he heard the buzzing of all kinds of rumors about the wolf. What Francis heard was enough to anger most creatures. He was glad that the wolf could not understand human speech, because he remembered how desolate and depressed he felt when he first changed his way of life and his fellow Assisians had mocked and jeered him. He immediately felt a deeper solidarity and connection to this wolf than to the terrified citizens of Gubbio.[67]

Francis understood the virtue of being non-judgmental. He understood that in a conflict, every side has a narrative, every side has erred and been harmed, and both sides want the hope and possibility of peace. For fear of his safety, the townspeople pleaded with Francis not to go outside the gate to confront the wolf. Francis felt that he had to go into the forest to communicate in some way with the starving and desperate wolf.

With the townspeople behind him, Francis walked outside of the city's gate into the forest. He called out to the wolf to come and meet in peace. Francis' call was a call to begin the process of healing in the moment, of listening to the other, and of wanting to understand why there was such aggressive and brazen behavior.

Francis saw the wolf, who was baring its teeth and growling. The crowd stood motionless and silent. Francis stared at the wolf. Anger flashed in the wolf's eyes and he was working his jaws. Francis dared not move, but he said in a simple, low, quiet voice, "Brother Wolf." The wolf quieted down in an apparent response. Francis felt the loneliness of the wolf and his suffering. He realized that the wolf was starving, and when it sought food among the flocks, the wolf encountered shepherds seeking to protect the flock. From there, tension and aggression escalated on both sides, with fear and hunger dictating the next steps.[68]

Then Francis talked with the wolf, referring to him as "Brother Wolf." He presented the wolf with a peace pact between him and the townspeople where he agreed not to harm them anymore and in exchange, they would give him food every day as long as he lived, so that he would never suffer from hunger. Then all the people who were assembled there promised in a loud voice to feed the wolf regularly. Francis stretched out his hand. The wolf seemed calm, but he remained immobile, scanning the crowd with his large, bloodshot eyes. Then slowly he walked to Francis and lifted his paw into Francis' warm, steady hand. The two remained in that position for a long time, and what Francis said to the wolf, he never told to anyone. Finally, Francis leaned over and put his arms about the wolf's neck.[69]

From that day, the wolf and the people kept the pact that Francis made between them. The wolf lived two years more, and he went from door to door for food. The people welcomed him as a beloved citizen. He hurt no one, and no one hurt him. The people fed him courteously. Then the wolf grew old and died. According to tradition, the people of Gubbio gave the wolf an honorable burial and later built the Church of Saint Francis of the Peace at the site. During a renovation of the church in 1872, the skeleton of a large wolf, apparently several centuries old, was found under a slab near the church wall and then reburied inside.

When we meet our fears this way, we develop the ability to become allies instead of enemies, like the wolf and the villagers. It is not a magical snap of the fingers, but a work of love, which can risk all for the sake of the vulnerable. At the heart of this story is the willingness and capacity to enter, with humility, into the heart of conflict in order to create a place that is sacred, hospitable, and healing, and where hope can grow and take root in the lives of all people.

Walking into and addressing conflict in this nonviolent way does not mean that we must stop the work of dismantling oppressive systems and institutions that exploit, abuse and degrade classes of people. As activists we fight against these unjust systems every day. But at the same time, we must offer to those who perpetuate these systems the opportunity to give up their unjust and cruel acts, be it in business, political positions, organizations or family settings. We can invite them to treat all others with the respect and dignity that they would ask for themselves. Even for the ones that refuse to change their ways, we must treat with kindness and compassion, as we rigorously challenge their unjust system and the culture that supports it.

A Great Wagon
by Rumi[70]

Out beyond ideas of wrongdoing and right-
doing,
there is a field. I'll meet you there.
When the soul lies down in that grass,
the world is too full to talk about.
Ideas, language, even the phrase "each
other"
doesn't make any sense.
The breeze at dawn has secrets to tell you.
Don't go back to sleep.
You must ask for what you really want.
Don't go back to sleep.
People are going back and forth across the
doorsill
where the two worlds touch.
The door is round and open.
Don't go back to sleep.

Your Reflections On Chapter 8:

Chapter 9

Do not try to be loved, but to love.

Francis teaches us the living way of striving towards unconditional love. He teaches us to try to find this love in our daily interactions and relationships. During his time, Francis chose the company of lepers in the leper colonies on the outskirts of the cities to provide them with healing and comfort. Whether it be in the company of the homeless, lepers, or other outcasts, Francis chose to live among them daily. Francis was a tough, demanding revolutionary voyager of the human spirit. He chose to live not with the easy metaphors of poverty, but to deeply embrace the poor and suffering of his society.

Francis had a relentless emphasis on genuine compassion and its necessary companion, humility as the expressions of his love. His life (rather than his words) teaches us what it is like to live in unconditional service of others.

As activists, we must strive to find the humanity in and connect with persons involved in our daily tasks or activities. Loving yourself is instrumental for the sake of loving others. We must love ourselves and to accept who we are as unique and special in the work for justice. The companion expressions of love walk together hand in hand. Francis saw love as a universal force in each of us that forms the thread connecting us all.

For our work, we must tap into this universal love for ourselves. We cannot do the work for justice and loving others if we don't have peace and love in our hearts. With all the examples of the life of Francis, along with his wise words, I have come to learn that compassion is not easy or painless; it is life's most demanding work. It is an essential virtue in the work for justice.

Francis believed that compassion, if it has any meaning at all, needs to be translated into action. The best example of how Francis embraced a life of compassion and service was his experience with lepers.

During the Middle Ages, there was no cure for leprosy. The practice in those days was to isolate lepers into their own colonies that were quarantined by society. The thought was that this isolation would help prevent the spread of the disease. For most of history, people with leprosy suffered alone in these isolated colonies, shut off by society.

Francis grew up with a strong distaste for lepers. He grew up in what would be the equivalent of the 1% today. His father was a wealthy merchant who made a fortune in the emerging mercantile economy that would eventually replace the one based on the feudalism of the Middle Ages. It was said that the young Francis would look at the houses of lepers from two miles away and would hold up his nostrils with his fingers in disgust.[71]

One day Francis came across a leper on the road while riding his horse. He felt all the discomfort and feeling of nausea as he got closer to the leper.

Instead of riding away and evading the encounter however, a strange feeling inside made Francis stay on the path towards the leper. He got off his horse, walked up to the leper and kissed him on the cheek.[72] Soon thereafter, Francis would move to the leper colony and begin caring for them and washing their wounds.

Something powerful happened when Francis got off his horse and kissed the leper. He went outside of his comfort zone and reached out with love and compassion to a person in an unfamiliar situation. He listened to his heart and connected with the leper's heart instead of giving in to his fears and doubts. This small act of compassion was the beginning of a life journey for Francis rooted in the teachings of the Gospel that started a movement for peace. Whenever Francis would see a poor person, he would reach out with unconditional love and compassion.

In her first book *Emergent Strategy: Shaping Change, Changing Worlds*, social justice facilitator, writer, artist, healer, and doula adrienne marie brown offers insights and inspiration during countless moments of tragedy and crisis. *Emergent Strategy* is a lyrical, explorative, non-linear journey of the book's title, a concept brown defines as "how we intentionally change in ways that grow our capacity to embody the just and liberated worlds we long for."[73] brown challenges us to know that our existence--who and how we are--is in and of itself a contribution to the people and place around us.

By bringing ourselves fully into a space, we are contributing with our presence. We do not need to do some particular thing to contribute, but bringing ourselves fully into a space will create a strong interconnectedness that can lead to collective transformation. Our quality of life and our survival are tied to how authentic and generous are the connections between us and the people and places in which we live. By practicing generosity and vulnerability, we can make these connections between us and others clear, open, available, and durable. Generosity here means giving of what we have without strings or expectations attached. Vulnerability means expressing what we need at any moment.[74]

Human beings, especially the ones who persist in trying to transform the living conditions of others, are remarkably resilient. We experience so much loss, pain, hardship, and attacks – and yet, we persist. Resilience is in our nature. Again and again, we recover from things that could justify our giving up. Resilience is unveiled when we are triggered by trauma, injured, heartbroken, attacked, challenged. Our general resilience as social justice activists in a traumatizing world and as collectives of people shaping the future is embedded in transformative justice, transforming the conditions that make injustice possible. Resilience is perhaps our most beautiful trait.[75]

From her perspectives on resilience, adrienne marie brown calls on us to adopt peace as the most strategic option for our long-term survival. She argues for a shared vision of an uncompromising peace where, through finding the places of healing and transformation, we move towards a world beyond enemies. The process for this approach is what she defines as "transformative justice" – justice that transforms the root causes of injustice at every scale, but especially on how it becomes the common orientation and practice of movements for social change and liberation.[76]

It is through compassion where we are able to live and experience each other's joy, happiness, grief and difficulties. Compassion begins with a communication that is genuine and heart to heart (not mind to mind). It involves speaking from the heart and actively listening from the heart. Acting with compassion as an activist is not taking a passive position or accepting the cruelty and oppression created by unjust systems and institutions. In our work to dismantle the injustices caused by oppressive systems and institutions, we also have to reach out and try to win over those persons seduced by the wealth and power perpetuated by them.

Thomas Merton (1915 - 1968), was an American Trappist monk, writer, theologian, mystic, poet, social justice activist, interfaith leaders and scholar of comparative religion. He was "a spiritual master" to millions of people around the world. Merton was a deep archivist of all his life experiences. He processed all his reading and encounters with others through many books, letters and daily journals. Of all his works, the one I relish the most is *New Seeds of Contemplation*,[77] one of his most widely read and best-loved books. For me, this book has nurtured my awareness of the contemplative presence in my daily work for justice.

Merton was a pioneer in recognizing the value of contemplation *and* action. He teaches us that our inner spiritual disciplines are connected to our outer service in the world. By performing my daily work in contemplation, I deepen my experience of service. I find purpose and meaning in every task and activity, and how they connect to the lives of others. I find humanity in every task.

Merton tells us that "every moment and every event of every person's life on earth plants something in their soul. For just as the wind carries thousands of winged seeds, so each moment brings with it germs of spiritual vitality that come to rest imperceptibly in our minds and wills. Most of these unnumbered seeds perish and are lost, because we are not prepared to receive them: for such seeds as these cannot spring up anywhere except in the soil of freedom, spontaneity and love."[78]

When Thomas Merton speaks of the contemplative life, he does not mean the institutional cloistered life. He is talking about a special dimension of inner discipline and experience, a certain integrity and fullness of personal development. This experience is not disconnected from our daily work and existence. Instead, contemplation enables us to connect with our creativity and capacity to integrate love and compassion in our work. They all come together.

For Thomas Merton, true solitude is to become deeply aware of the world's needs. It does not hold the world at arm's length. It brings us to unity with the world.[79] Merton teaches us that as social justice activists, we must make time for solitude in order to find the gentleness inside us. We can then integrate back into the work with deeper love and compassion for others.[80]

A certain depth of the contemplative experience as described by Merton can become a way for social justice activists to deepen solidarity when engaged in an activity, protest or mobilization. Oftentimes, our daily work for justice can tend to be superficial and deceptive. Without a more profound human understanding derived from a process like the contemplative experience, we can lose the essence of love and compassion in our work. Prayer, meditation and contemplation are tools that we can apply daily to deepen our personal lives and expand our capacity to serve others with love, compassion and understanding.

Love's Exquisite Freedom
by Maya Angelou[81]

We, unaccustomed to courage
exiles from delight
live coiled in shells of loneliness
until love leaves its high holy temple
and comes into our sight
to liberate us into life.

Love arrives
and in its train come ecstasies
old memories of pleasure
ancient histories of pain.
Yet if we are bold,
love strikes away the chains of fear
from our souls.

We are weaned from our timidity
In the flush of love's light
we dare be brave
And suddenly we see
that love costs all we are
and will ever be.
Yet it is only love
which sets us free.

Your Reflections On Chapter 9:

Chapter 10

Because it is in giving that we receive.

In the work for justice, we must approach the giving and receiving as one and the same. When we give with an expectation of receiving something in return – praise, recognition, a favor or ask—we shift from our genuine loving self to our ego-centered self. The moment of joy should be in the giving, as the other person shares a joy in the receiving. They should become one in the same. The person giving and the person receiving share the same moment of joy that unites them both. Both are receiving and giving in that one special moment.

Whenever I reflect on this verse of the Prayer for Peace, Roberto Vargas and his teachings come to mind. Vargas is a spiritual activist, educator and consultant, nationally recognized for his exceptional skills in providing leadership coaching and creating interactive environments. Vargas helps multicultural groups achieve high levels of creativity and success. In his groundbreaking book, *Family Activism: Empowering Your Community, Beginning with Family and Friends*, Vargas introduces us to *PorVida Living,* his spiritual approach to community building in his work for justice. *PorVida* is being for life, love, respect, and justice. It is the daily approach to live, work, and guide with the intent of being a better person and advancing a healthy society and world for all.[82]

Reconnecting with your *PorVida* essence deepens your understanding of your life purpose. It is the best way to stay on course and inspired, reconnecting with spirit, purpose and love. Tapping into your *PorVida* essence nurtures your spirit to make your living purpose joyful and connect you with your power.[83]

This process will be different for every activist, but Vargas encourages us to find ways to connect with spirit and then develop our own practices for nurturing the reconnection. The activist preparation of connecting with spirit is sometimes called grounding, because you are fortifying your connection with that which nurtures you, like a tree that drives its roots deeper into the ground to ensure its sustenance.[84]

For Vargas, the giving and receiving of our *PorVida* essence involves the process of co-powering communication.[85] This involves giving love and support to others and at the same time humbly and gratefully accepting the opportunity to be of service. As activists desiring a better world, our power is exponentially greater when we share our *PorVida* nature with others and receive theirs in return. Our role as activists is to both embrace our *PorVida* nature and pursue our success, while we also help others recognize their inherent goodness and realize their potential. Co-powering communication is consciously seeking to uplift the confidence and power of others for the mutual good that can result.[86] This power process of solidarity and relationship building creates strong community by uplifting the confidence and power of everyone around us, particularly our supporters and potential allies.

Francis had a deep *PorVida* nature. For him, the giving and receiving must be unconditional. It is just as important to receive as to give, and vice versa. Francis teaches us that we are always in community in the work for justice. This is true co-powerment in action. We give to one another, but we must also receive from one another. The giving and receiving become one in the same.

Blessing in the Chaos
  by Jan Richardson[87]

To all that is chaotic

in you,
let there come silence.

Let there be
a calming
of the clamoring,
a stilling
of the voices that
have laid their claim
on you,
that have made their
home in you,

that go with you
even to the
holy places
but will not
let you rest,
will not let you
hear your life
with wholeness
or feel the grace
that fashioned you.

Let what distracts you
cease.

Let what divides you
cease.
Let there come an end
to what diminishes
and demeans,
and let depart
all that keeps you
in its cage.

Let there be
an opening
into the quiet
that lies beneath
the chaos,
where you find
the peace
you did not think
possible
and see what shimmers
within the storm.

Your Reflections On Chapter 10:

Chapter 11

It is in forgiving that we are forgiven.

When you forgive someone, you are not forgetting or excusing the act that caused you a harm or injustice. You are not pardoning or condoning the act. Nor are you abandoning the fight to confront and dismantle the injustice caused by the act. To forgive is powerful. It is an act of courage, where you decide to no longer hold anger or bitterness towards a person. It is an act of liberation, because you are no longer bound by the anger that the person caused you to hold. It is an emotional release and liberation.[88]

Anger and bitterness towards a person can lead to personal hate, which will destroy your mind, body and soul. Forgiveness enables you to no longer relive the incident and to no longer feel again the blistering anger.

Nor does forgiving someone mean that you have to reconnect with that person. Many times it will be unwise to do so. Forgiving simply means that you no longer hold the person in your negative thoughts, filled with anger and bitterness. It is your moment to heal and bring justice to yourself.

Francis in his approach to forgiveness can teach us a lot about integrating this important virtue in our work for justice A forgiving heart is an important part of activism. An unforgiving spirit blocks the flow of grace and mercy into our lives. It causes us to live in a stagnant state of regrets, animosities and grudges. Francis teaches us that forgiveness creates room in your heart for love and mercy, which are necessary for bringing peace in the world.

Desmond Tutu connects us with the African wisdom tradition of Ubuntu. It is a Nguni Bantu term meaning "humanity." It is often translated as "I am because we are," or "humanity towards others," or in Xhosa, "umntu ngumntu ngabantu." It is often used in a more philosophical sense to mean, "the belief in a universal bond of sharing that connects all humanity." For Desmond Tutu, it speaks of the very essence of being human. When we want to give high praise to someone we say, "Yu, u nobunto" or "Hey so-and-so has *ubuntu*."[89]

From the perspective of Ubuntu, a person is a person through other persons. Once we have accepted ourselves, our vulnerabilities, and our humanity, we can accept the humanity of others. We can have compassion for our faults and have compassion for those of others. We can be generous and give our joy to others. According to Desmond Tutu, "It is when without thinking about it you help someone who is less well off, when you are kind to someone else and do those things that raise others up, you end up being joyful. Joy is the reward, really, of seeking to give joy to others."[90]

When you show compassion, when you show caring, when you show love to others, do things for others, in a wonderful way you have a deep joy that you can get in no other way. Ubuntu is a way of life that acknowledges that every person is of infinite value. In other words, we need one another in order to each discover our beauty and allow it to shine by what we do with our lives. As Desmond Tutu teaches, "A person is only a person in the context of other persons: my humanity is caught up, is inextricably bound up, in yours."[91]

Nelson Mandela can be considered a true example of Ubuntu, as he used this concept to lead South Africa to a peaceful post-apartheid society. He never had the intention of exacting vengeance and teaching his oppressors a lesson. Instead, he operated with compassion and integrity, showing many in his country that for a better South Africa, they must not act out of vengeance or retaliation, but out of peace.[92] "We think of ourselves far too frequently as just individuals, separated from one another, whereas you are connected and what you do affects the whole world," Desmond Tutu said. "When you do well, it spreads out; it is for the whole of humanity."[93]

This is exactly what Ubuntu is about, it's a reminder that no one is an island — every single thing that you do, good or bad, has an effect on your family, friends, and society. It also reminds us that we need to think twice about the choices we want to make and the kind of impact they may have on others.

By practicing Ubuntu in our daily lives, we can learn that hatred is not innate; that in the work to eliminate white supremacy and institutions of oppression, we must also reach out and try to transform individuals. The lessons of Ubuntu challenge us to overcome the stereotypes and mistaken beliefs that we have about each other so that we can connect as allies in the quest for racial justice.[94] Ubuntu is about togetherness, as well as a fight for the greater good. It is the belief that everyone in society needs to play a part, regardless of how small one may think it is. We all have a role to play, and it's of vital importance that our actions inspire others to want to be a part of a better and brighter future. This is what Mandela was prepared to sacrifice his life for.

The Well of Grief
by David Whyte[95]

Those who will not slip beneath
the still surface on the well of grief,

turning down through its black water
to the place we cannot breathe,

will never know the source from which we drink,
the secret water, cold and clear,

nor find in the darkness glimmering,

the small round coins,
thrown by those who wished for something else.

Your Reflections On Chapter 11:

Chapter 12

And it is in dying that we are
born to eternal life.

Francis' work and the movement that he created during his lifetime brought a new perspective to Catholicism – to bring about the kingdom of heaven here on earth. Eight centuries ago, Francis was trying to create a society analogous to the "Beloved Community" envisioned by Dr. Martin Luther King Jr. during the Civil Rights Movement of the 1960's. The concept of the Beloved Community originated in the early days of the 20th Century by the philosopher-theologian Josiah Royce, who founded the Fellowship of Reconciliation. However, it was Dr. King, also a member of that Fellowship, who popularized the term and invested it with a deeper meaning which has captured the imagination of social justice activists all over the world.[96]

Dr. King's Beloved Community is a global vision in which all people can share in the wealth of the earth. In the Beloved Community, poverty, hunger and homelessness will not be tolerated because international standards of human decency will not allow it. Racism and all forms of discrimination, bigotry and prejudice will be replaced by an all-inclusive spirit of sisterhood and brotherhood.

In the Beloved Community, international disputes will be resolved by peaceful conflict-resolution and reconciliation of adversaries, instead of military power. Love and trust will triumph over fear and hatred. Peace with justice will prevail over war and military conflict.[97]

Francis teaches us to deal with conflicts and disagreements based on compassion, understanding, gentleness, and love. He did not see the world in terms of good vs. bad or saints vs. sinners. Instead, he saw the world as every human being deserving of love and respect. Francis' approach to compassionate living is a life of non-violence and instilling this virtue in others.

In his 1963 sermon, *Loving Your Enemies*, published in his book, *Strength to Love*, Dr. King addressed the role of unconditional love in struggling for the Beloved Community: "With every ounce of our energy we must continue to rid this nation of the incubus of segregation. But we shall not in the process relinquish our privilege and our obligation to love. While abhorring segregation, we shall love the segregationist. This is the only way to create the beloved community."[98]

Francis died and was born to eternal life when he left his youthful ego-centered life of pleasure, renounced his worldly goods and stood naked in front of his parents in the plaza square. This decision was the turning point in his life to shift from an ego-centered lifestyle to one rooted in the Gospel teachings of love, understanding and compassion.

In our work for peace and justice, our ability to shift from our ego-centered self to genuine love and compassion enables us to be fully alive in the present moment as we engage in our work with peace inside our hearts. We die spiritually when we act from our ego-centered selves and lose our true essence of community and solidarity. We encounter a rebirth every day when we embrace and act from a place of love, compassion, understanding and radical solidarity.

When we turn away from the part of us that separates us from others – our individual desires, our self-interests, the attitudes and emotions like envy and jealousy that build walls around us – and come alive to the part of us that we share in common with others – our compassion and understanding, our capacity for service, our caring for all of creation – we are able to embrace the world and become one with the hearts of those we meet. It is a rare and delicate balance, for we can never truly be free of our own sense of self. But we can recognize that if we strive to divest ourselves of our own self-centeredness and its demands, then we truly are open to the world and the wonders it contains. When we listen to someone with our hearts, not to offer advice but to be fully present to their joy, fears and dreams, when we give selflessly of our time or energy to be there for someone in need, these are the times we are forsaking our ego-centered self and coming alive to our beloved community. For we live on in the hearts and minds of people we struggled with, fought battles together, lifted them up and helped them carry on. As they remember us and embody our ideals, we live on through them.

The work for justice is never ending. It is in a continuum. Francis was rooted in servant leadership. For him, stepping back and out of the way for others to emerge as leaders of his movement was at the core of his leadership role. Francis worked daily not only to be in the service of others, but also to cultivate the next generation to take on his work. We create the harvest of the future with the seeds that we plant today. In our daily work for justice, we create an imprint in humanity that enables us to be present in the work for justice long after we depart this lifetime. We leave behind the work for justice that continues in those who carry on the torch after we leave. While Francis believed in an eternal life in heaven after death, he also struggled with creating a heaven on earth, a just society where all are valued and cared for. Those of us in the work for social justice can find solace and comfort in knowing we are each playing our own part in creating that just society, our heaven on earth.

The Summer Day
by Mary Oliver[99]

Who made the world?
Who made the swan, and the black bear?
Who made the grasshopper?
This grasshopper, I mean—
the one who has flung herself out of the
grass,
the one who is eating sugar out of my hand,
who is moving her jaws back and forth
instead of up and down—
who is gazing around with her enormous
and complicated eyes.
Now she lifts her pale forearms and thor-
oughly washes her face.
Now she snaps her wings open, and floats
away.
I don't know exactly what a prayer is.
I do know how to pay attention, how to fall
down
into the grass, how to kneel down in the
grass,
how to be idle and blessed, how to stroll
through the fields,
which is what I have been doing all day.
Tell me, what else should I have done?
Doesn't everything die at last, and too
soon?
Tell me, what is it you plan to do
with your one wild and precious life?

Your Reflections On Chapter 12:

Chapter 13

Addressing Climate Change in the Work for Justice

The crisis of climate change exerts a powerful impact on all of us today. The looming catastrophes often feel overwhelming in their depth and complexity. We have seen its destruction of habitats and ecosystems across the entire planet.

Pope Francis has been a leading voice in fighting the climate crisis. Prior to the drafting of the UN Paris Climate Agreement in 2015, Pope Francis published *Laudato Si: On Care of Our Common Home,* his encyclical on climate change.[100] In *Laudato Si,* Pope Francis combines fighting for the well-being of the earth with economic justice and a call to treat all human beings with dignity and respect. Much in the spirit of Francis of Assisi, He shows us just how inseparable the bond is between concern for nature, justice for the poor, commitment to society, and internal peace.

Among the major teachings of this encyclical is how the poor are disproportionately affected by climate change. We as human beings must be united by the concern for our planet, and every living thing that dwells on it, especially the poorest and most vulnerable. With the rich countries hurting the poor countries, the encyclical calls for a "more balanced level of production, a better distribution of wealth, concern for the environment and the rights of future generations."[101]

At heart, this document, addressed to "every person on the planet" is a call for a new way of looking at things, a "bold cultural revolution."[102] Today, we are facing an urgent crisis when, thanks to our actions, the earth has begun to look more and more like, in Pope Francis' vivid language, "an immense pile of filth."[103] Still, the document is hopeful. It reminds us that because God is with us, or for some, that our faith that we can make a better world for all is in us, we can strive both individually and collectively to change course. We can awaken our hearts and move towards an "ecological conversion" in which we see the intimate connection between the spiritual dimension or the sublime and all beings, in which we more readily listen to the "cry of the earth and the cry of the poor."[104]

Francis of Assisi's Canticle of the Creatures is a poem that he created during his final days when he was seriously ill and blind. This poem was his expression from the depths of his inner core. It is an extension of Francis' depth of humanity to the rest of creation and natural elements. Through this poem, Francis expresses his interconnectedness and service to all of creation and nature. Through it, Francis embraces and promotes the dignity and respect for all creatures, plants, natural elements, heavens and the earth. He expresses his deep solidarity with all creatures, trees, plants, and natural environments as sisters and brothers. Below is the part of the poem that describes how Francis relished in the love for Brother Sun, Sister Moon and Stars, Brother Wind and Air, Sister Water, Brother Fire, and Mother Earth:

Praised be my Lord God with all your creatures,
especially our Brother Sun,
who brings us the day and who brings us the light.
Fair is he and shines with a very great splendor:
O Lord, he signifies you to us!

Praised be You, Most High, for Sister Moon and the Stars,
You set them in the heavens, making them so bright, luminous and fine.

Praised be my Lord for our Brother Wind,
and for air and cloud, calms and all weather
through which you uphold life in all creatures.

Praised be my Lord for our Sister Water,
who is very useful and humble
and precious and clean.

Praised be my Lord for Brother Fire,
through whom you give us light in the darkness;
and he is bright and pleasant and very mighty
and strong.

Praised be my Lord, for our Mother Earth,
who does sustain and keep us,
and brings forth many fruits and flowers
of many colors, and grass.[105]

In his powerful little book, *The World We Have: A Buddhist Approach to Peace and Ecology*, Thich Nhat Hanh talks about how we can embrace the concept of "impermanence" and its practice to understand our interconnectedness with our body, ourselves and all in the earth. He describes how we are destroying the earth and ourselves by not caring for our earth, her creatures and her resources that sustain us. He refers to global warming as an early symptom leading us to the death of our planet.[106]

Impermanence involves an awareness of all things in endless transformation. When we are able to look deeply at a flower, a leaf, or a living being, we can see the change taking place in every instant. When we look deeply at cyclic change and see that it is a necessary part of life, we do not suffer so deeply when it occurs. We look deeply at the impermanence of our own body, the impermanence of the things around us, the impermanent nature of the people we love and the impermanent nature of those who cause us to suffer.[107]

Impermanence also means interdependence. A flower is always receiving non-flower elements, such as water, air, and sunshine, and it's always giving something back to the environment. A flower is a stream of change, and a person is also a stream of change. At every instant, there is an input and output. A flower is always being born and always dying, always connected to the environment around it. The components of the universe depend on others for their existence.[108] When we fight against the nature of impermanence, we suffer. We can allow our fears, anger, and despair to overwhelm us. That is why it is very important to deal with our fear and despair before we can deal with the issue of global warming and other environmental concerns. We have to heal ourselves first before we can heal the planet.[109] We need a paradigm shift in the way we integrate the climate crisis into our work for justice. We breath the same air; we drink the same water; we experience the light of the same sun. We are all interconnected through Mother Earth.

Saint Francis had a deep affection for all of creation. He felt great joy in contemplating the power, wisdom and goodness of the Creator in all creatures. It was with this joy that he looked upon the stars and beheld the moon, picked up little worms on the road to prevent them from being trampled on, and had a special love for the flowers.[110]

Of course, there is the famous story of Francis preaching to the birds, which has become an iconic world symbol and statute in many of our gardens. Francis addressed them all as sisters and brothers. Francis showed us the interconnectedness with all of nature.[111]

Francis teaches us to open our eyes and hearts not just to one another, but to all of creation. The well-being of our earth and bio-diversity is an important component of fighting for justice in the world. Francis helps us to see that an integral ecology calls for openness to categories which transcend the language of mathematics and biology, and take us to the heart of what it is to be human. Just as happens when we fall in love with someone, whenever he would gaze at the sun, the moon or the smallest of animals, he burst into song, drawing all other creatures into his praise.

The quality that has connected St. Francis to many of us throughout the centuries is his unwavering love for nature and all creatures. He saw our connection and appreciation for all of creation as instrumental to a life of joy on earth. Francis saw his deep and loving presence with creation as heaven on earth, and we are called to be peacemakers to bring justice and peace in the world, to heal Mother Earth, even as we find healing in our love for one another. And for ourselves.

Pale Blue Dot:
A Vision of the Human Future in Space
by Carl Sagan

This 2013 image from NASA's Cassini space-craft features Earth as a speck, and recalls Carl Sagan's Pale Blue Dot message from 1990 that is a must read today as we live with so many crises and so much uncertainty:

"Look again at that dot. That's here. That's home. That's us. On it everyone you love, everyone you know, everyone you ever heard of, every human being who ever was, lived out their lives. The aggregate of our joy and suffering, thousands of confident religions, ideologies, and economic doctrines, every hunter and forager, every hero and coward, every creator and destroyer of civilization, every king and peasant, every young couple in love, every mother and father, hopeful child, inventor and explorer, every teacher of morals, every corrupt politician, every "superstar," every "supreme leader," every saint and sinner in the history of our species lived there-on a mote of dust suspended in a sunbeam.

The Earth is a very small stage in a vast cosmic arena. Think of the endless cruelties visited by the inhabitants of one corner of this pixel on the scarcely distinguishable inhabitants of some other corner, how frequent their misunderstandings, how eager they are to kill one another, how fervent their hatreds. Think of the rivers of blood spilled by all those generals and emperors so that, in glory and triumph, they could become the momentary masters of a fraction of a dot.

Our posturing, our imagined self-importance, the delusion that we have some privileged position in the Universe, are challenged by this point of pale light. Our planet is a lonely speck in the great enveloping cosmic dark. In our obscurity, in all this vastness, there is no hint that help will come from elsewhere to save us from ourselves.

The Earth is the only world known so far to harbor life. There is nowhere else, at least in the near future, to which our species could migrate. Visit, yes. Settle, not yet. Like it or not, for the moment the Earth is where we make our stand.

It has been said that astronomy is a humbling and character-building experience. There is perhaps no better demonstration of the folly of human conceits than this distant image of our tiny world. To me, it underscores our responsibility to deal more kindly with one another, and to preserve and cherish the pale blue dot, the only home we've ever known."[112]

Your Reflections On Chapter 13:

Final thoughts

I hope you have enjoyed this book and our journey through it together. May you continue forward with your spiritual journey so it can grow to become an inherent part of your life as an activist for justice. Francis' way of peacemaking is expressing love in action in the work for justice. Love is fluid in this work. Our existence depends on it. We need awareness of love at all times, especially during moments of chaos and crisis. We can easily forget that we are interconnected and we lose our compass. We fail to see beyond the idiosyncrasies.

Beyond me and you, love appears. Love "re-members" us as one. Love is endless, it is not finite, you can never give or receive more than enough of it. It has no limits. In the work for justice, our love for one another is the deepest form of solidarity. It brings us back together, acknowledges and nurtures us.

When you love for the act of loving itself, peace will fill your heart, and this will be the same for the other person. Love is the giving and receiving.

Francis found love in the present moment. He saw every moment as a pathway to deepen his five senses to be fully presence in love. For Francis, love was in his body and in whatever surrounded him in the present moment. He could always count on love being there for the taking. As activists for social justice, if we are able to give and receive love, we will be love in action and be loved. Justice is about bringing love to others. Love is doing justice in the world.

Finally, I leave you with an excerpt from a teaching from the great Jewish thinker, Rabbi Tarfon, as translated by Rabbi Rami Shapiro.[113] I always share this piece with my UCLA students during my last day of class with them:

> You are not obligated to complete the work,
>> but neither are you free to abandon it.
>
> Do not be daunted
> by the enormity of the world's grief.
> Do justly, now.
> Love mercy, now.
> Walk humbly, now.

About the Author

A nationally known expert on immigrant rights and low-wage workers, Victor Narro has been involved with immigrant rights and labor issues for over 35 years. Currently Victor is Project Director for the UCLA Labor Center and Core Faculty for the UCLA Labor Studies Program and the Public Interest Law Program of UCLA Law School. He is co-editor of *Broken Laws, Unprotected Workers: Violations of Employment and Labor Laws in America's Cities* (2008); *Wage Theft and Workplace Violations in Los Angeles* (2010); *Undocumented and Unafraid: Tam Tran, Cinthya Felix, and the Immigrant Youth Movement* (UCLA Center for Labor Research and Education, 2012); and *Mike Garcia and The Justice for Janitors Movement* (UCLA Center for Labor Research and Education, 2020). He is co-editor of *Working for Justice: The L.A. Model of Organizing and Advocacy* (Cornell University Press, 2010) and *No One Size Fits All: Worker Organization, Policy, and Movement in a New Economic Age* (Cornell University Press, 2018). Victor has published a children's book entitled *Jimmy's Carwash Adventure* (Hard Ball Press, 2016). In addition to his work at the UCLA Labor Center, Victor is a Movement Chaplain with Faith Matters Network and a SoulCollage® Facilitator. Victor is happily married to Laureen Lazarovici, a long-time labor activist and journalist.

Epilogue

Victor Narro has been a good friend and colleague at the UCLA Labor Center for nearly twenty years. His pathbreaking work to infuse spirituality and self-kindness within labor and social justice movements has had a profound impact. Victor has taught us that we activists must take care of ourselves. We can't separate our political lives from our personal lives, and we must promote thoughtful self-care to avoid burn-out that can lead to dropping out of the movement.

The work of an activist is physically and emotionally demanding. Yet it is a calling that can bring great joy and fulfillment. Victor is regularly called on to assist unions, worker centers, and community organizations to strengthen their work through spirituality and self-kindness. He has also taught courses at UCLA which helped to prepare our students for a life of activism.

On December 11, 2021, the UCLA Labor Center dedicated our building in Los Angeles in honor of Rev. James Lawson Jr. It is appropriate that this is the very building where Victor has worked for the past two decades. Rev. Lawson worked closely with Dr. Martin Luther King Jr. on the Nashville Sit-In campaign and the Memphis Sanitation Workers strike, and has had a historic impact in infusing the philosophy of nonviolence to the U.S. experience.

We recently published a new book with Rev. Lawson entitled Revolutionary Nonviolence: Organizing for Freedom (UC Press, 2021.) Victor's new book The Activist Spirit aligns well with Rev. Lawson's teachings on nonviolence. Here is a quote from Rev. Lawson in Revolutionary Nonviolence:

"So where do we go from here? I think that the most important soil that you and I must cultivate is to lay the seeds for the movements of the twenty-first century that will reclaim democracy for the United States, that will reclaim justice, reclaim equality, reclaim liberty for all in the United States. I think that we have to lay the seeds by which we can take government out of the hands of the oligarchy and out of the hands of the military and put it back into the hands of truth and the beloved community. That needs to be our goal in the twenty-first century, and I think that it's a goal that we can achieve if all around the country ordinary people get involved in it."

We hope that these two important books will inspire generations to come to join our movement for peace and human liberation.

Kent Wong is the director of the UCLA Labor Center, and has been a good friend and colleague of Victor Narro for the past two decades.

Endnotes

1   Leonardo Boff, *Francis of Assisi* (New York: Orbis Books, 1982).

2   Ibid., 106.

3   Jon M. Sweeney, *Lord, Make Me and Instrument of Your Peace: The Complete Prayers of St. Francis, St. Clare & other early Franciscans* (Brewster, MA: Paraclete Press, 2020).

4   Ibid., 259.

5   Mario T. Garica, *The Gospel of César Chávez: My Faith in Action* (Lanham MD: Sheed & Ward, 2007), 8-9.

6   Ibid.

7   Jon M. Sweeney, *The St. Francis Holy Fool Prayer Book* (Brewster, MA: Paraclete Press, 2017), 31.

8   Martha Postlethwaite, "Clearing" in Mindfulness Association, accessed October 19, 2021,   https://www.mindfulnessassociation.net/words-of-wonder/clearing-martha-postlethwaite/

9   Paul Moses, *The Saint and The Sultan: The Crusades, Islam, and Francis of Assisi's Mission of Peace* (New York: Doubleday, 2009).

10   Ibid., 126-47.

11   Neringa Antanaityte, *Mind Matters: How To Effortlessly Have More Positive Thoughts*, TLEX Institute, accessed August 2021, https://tlexinstitute.com/how-to-effortlessly-have-more-positive-thoughts/

12   Jelaluddin Rumi, "The Guest House" in *Rumi: Selected Poems*, translated by Coleman Barks with John Moynce, A.J. Arberry, Reynold Nicholson (New York: Penguin Books, 2004), 109.

13   John Kirvan, *Peace of Heart: Francis of Assisi* (Notre Dame, IN: Ave Maria Press, 2009), 23-4.

14   Emily Shapiro, *Charleston Victim's Mother Tells Dylann Roof 'I Forgive You' as He's Sentenced to Death*, ABC News, January 11, 2017.

15   The Dalai Lama, Desmond Tutu and Douglas Abrams, *The Book of Joy: Lasting Happiness in a Changing World* (New York: Avery, 2016).

16   Ibid., 53.

17   Ibid., 229-39

18   Gina Sharpe, *The Power of Forgiveness*, Tricycle The Buddhist Review, Spring 2013, https://tricycle.org/magazine/power-forgiveness/

19   The Dalai Lama, Desmond Tutu and Douglas Abrams, 104-7.

20   Desmond Tutu and Mpho Tutu, "Prayer Before the Prayer." *The Book of Forgiving: The Fourfold Path for Healing Ourselves and Our World* (New York: Harper Collins, 2014), 6-7.

21   Br. David Steindl-Rast, *Gratefulness, the Heart of Prayer: An Approach to Life in Fullness* (Mahwah, NJ: Paulist Press, 1984).

22   Ibid., 23-5. See Also Br. David Steindl-Rast, *Want to be happy? Be grateful*, TEDGlobal, June 2013, https://www.ted.com/talks/david_steindl_rast_want_to_be_happy_be_grateful?language=en

23   Br. David Steindl-Rast, *Faith in Life,* A Network for Grateful Living, accessed March 2021, *https:// gratefulness.org/area-of-interest/faith-in-life/*

24   Ibid.

25   Br. David Steindl-Rast, *Gratefulness, the Heart of Prayer: An Approach to Life in Fullness*, 103-5.

26   Br. David Steindl-Rast, *Engaging Hope: Revolutionizing the Revolution. Engaging Hope with Br. David Steindl-Rast*, Spirituality & Practice, 2011, https:// www.spiritualityandpractice.com/ecourses/features/ view/24173/engaging-hope-with-br-david-steindl-rast

27   Ibid.

28   Ibid.

29   Ibid.

30   See *Theodore Parker And The 'Moral Universe',* All Things Considered – NPR, September 2, 2010, https://www.npr.org/templates/story/story. php?storyId=129609461

31   Br. David Steindl-Rast, *Gratefulness, the Heart of Prayer: An Approach to Life in Fullness*, 121-2.

32   Br. David Steindl-Rast, *Common Sense Spirituality* (New York: The Crossroad Publishing Company, 2008), 180-2.

33   Mary Oliver, "The Journey" in *Dream Work* (New York: Atlantic Monthly Press, 1986), 38.

34   Krista Tippet, *Becoming Wise: An Inquiry into the Mystery and Art of Living* (New York: Penguin Books, 2016).

35   Ibid., 233.

36   Ibid., 265-7.

37   Ibid., 233-8.

38   Thich Nhat Hanh, *Plum Village Chanting and Recitation Book* (Berkeley: Parallax Press, 2000), 68.

39   Thich Nhat Hanh, *Living Buddha, Living Christ* (New York: Riverhead Books, 2007), 83.

40   Jon M. Sweeney, *The St. Francis Holy Fool Prayer Book,* 41.

41   Jon. M. Sweeney, *Lord, Make Me and Instrument of Your Peace,* 38.

42   Danna Faulds, "Allow" in *Go In and In: Poems from the Heart of Yoga* (Peaceable Kingdom Books, 2002).

43   Ruby Sales, *Digital Interview* in The History-Makers, accessed March 2021, https://www.thehistorymakers.org/biography/ruby-nell-sales-39

44   Ruby Sales, *The SpiritHouse Project*, accessed March 15, 2021, http://www.spirithouseproject.org/about-spirithouse.php

45   Ibid.

46   Krista Tippet, *Ruby Sales Where Does It Hurt?,* On Being with Krista Tippett, accessed March 10, 2021, https://onbeing.org/programs/ruby-sales-where-does-it-hurt/

47   Ibid.

48   Ibid.

49   Robert H. Hopcke and Paul A. Schwarz, *The Little Flowers of Francis of Assisi: A New Translation* (Boston: New Seeds, 2006), 81.

50   Ibid., 84.

51   India.Arie, "I Am Light." Track 1 on SongVersation: Medicine. (BMG Rights Management (US) LLC, 2017), CD. See Also, India.Arie, "I Am Light." Genius, accessed October 19, 2021, https://genius.com/Indiaarie-i-am-light-lyrics.

52   John Kirvan, 91.

53   The Dalai Lama, Desmond Tutu and Douglas Abrams, 273-5.

54   Ibid., 270.

55   Thich Nhat Hanh, *Five Practices for Nurturing Happiness*, Lion's Roar, June 8, 2021, https://www.lionsroar.com/5-practices-for-nurturing-happiness/

56   Pema Chödrön, *How to Practice Tonglen*, Lion's Roar, June 8, 2021, https://www.lionsroar.com/how-to-practice-tonglen/

57   Ibid.

58   Pema Chödrön, *The Places That Scare You: A Guide to Fearlessness in Difficult Times* (New York: Shambhala Classics - Penguin Random House, 2005), 50.

59   Audre Lorde, "Coping" in *The Black Unicorn: Poems* (New York: W.W. Norton & Company, 1995), 45.

60   "Dorothy Day: 20th c. journalist and social activist who co-founded the Catholic Worker Movement." *A Vision of Justice.* Accessed March 1, 2021. https://faithandliberty.org/visions/dorothy-day

61   Ibid.

62   Ibid.

63   Leonardo Boff, 85.

64   Meister Eckhart, "The Hope of Loving" in *Love Poems from God: Twelve Sacred Voices from the East and West*, edited by Daniel Ladinsky (New York: Penguin Compass, 2002), 109.

65   Thich Nhat Hahn, *Living Buddha, Living Christ,* 20.

66   Murray Bodo, *Francis: The Journey and the Dream* (Cincinnati: St. Anthony Messenger Press, 2011), 77.

67   Ibid., 78.

68   Ibid.

69   Ibid., 81.

70   Jelaluddin Rumi, "A Great Wagon" in *Rumi: Selected Poems*, translated by Coleman Barks with John Moynce, A.J. Arberry, Reynold Nicholson (New York: Penguin Books, 2004), 35.

71   Murray Bodo, 16. See also André Vauchez, Francis of Assisi: The Life and Afterlife of a Medieval Saint (New Haven: Yale University Press, 2012), 22-5; Kirvan, Peace of Heart: Francis of Assisi, 26-7.

72   Ibid.

73   adrienne maree brown, *Emergent Strategy: Shaping Change, Changing Worlds* (Chico, CA: AK Press, 2017), 24.

74   Ibid., 142-3.

75   Ibid., 126.

76   Ibid., 132-33.

77   Thomas Merton, *New Seeds of Contemplation* (New York: New Directions Books, 2007).

78   Ibid., 14.

79   Jon M. Sweeney, *Thomas Merton: An Introduction to His Life, Teachings, and Practices* (New York: St. Martin's Essentials, 2021), 75.

80   Ibid., 32-3.

81   Maya Angelou, *Love's Exquisite Freedom* (New York: Welcome Books, 2011)

82   Roberto Vargas, *Family Activism: Empowering Your Community, Beginning with Family and Friends* (San Francisco: Berrett-Koehler Publishers, 2008)

83   Ibid., 76.

84   Ibid., 78.

85   Ibid., 107.

86   Ibid., 114-15.

87   Jan Richardson, "Blessing in the Chaos" in *The Cure for Sorrow: A Book of Blessings for Times of Grief* (Orlando, FL: Wanton Gospeller Press, 2016).

88   The Dalai Lama, Desmond Tutu and Douglas Abrams, 234-5.

89   Ibid., 60.

90   Ibid., 270-1.

91   Michael Battle, *The Wisdom of Desmond Tutu* (Oxford, England: Lion Publishing, 1998), 35.

92   Hlumelo Siphe Williams, *What Is the Spirit of Ubuntu? How Can We Have It in Our Lives?* https://www.globalcitizen.org/en/content/ubuntu-south-af-

rica-together-nelson-mandela/ (2018). See Also, The
Dalai Lama, Desmond Tutu and Douglas Abrams, *The
Book of Joy*, 43-5.

93   ClintonFoundation, *The Spirit of Ubuntu*.
https://stories.clintonfoundation.org/the-spirit-of-ubun-
tu-6f3814ab8596 (2012). See Also, The Dalai Lama,
Desmond Tutu and Douglas Abrams, *The Book of Joy*,
273-5.

94   Mark Mathabane, *The Lessons of Ubuntu: How
an African Philosophy Can Inspire Racial Healing in
America,* (New York: Skyhorse Publishing, 2018).

95   David Whyte, "The Well of Grief" in *River
Flow: New & Selected Poems* (Langley, WA: Many
Rivers Press, 2012).

96   The King Center, *The Beloved Community*,
https://thekingcenter.org/about-tkc/the-king-philosophy/

97   Ibid.

98   Dr. Martin Luther King, Jr., A Gift of Love:
Sermons from Strength to Love and Other Preachings
(Boston: Beacon Press, 2012), 53.

99

 Mary Oliver, "The Summer Day" in House of Light
(Boston: Beacon Press, 1990), 60.

100   Pope Francis, *Laudato Si*: On *Care of Our
Common Home* (Huntington, IN: Our Sunday Visitor,
2015).

101   Ibid., 37.

102   Ibid., 8, 78.

103   Ibid., 19.

104   Ibid., 34-5.

105   Jon. M. Sweeney, *Lord, Make Me and Instrument of Your Peace,* 170-1.

106   Thich Nhat Hanh, *The World We Have: A Buddhist Approach to Peace and Ecology* (Berkeley: Parallax Press, 2008).

107   Ibid., 44-45.

108   Ibid., 46.

109   Ibid., 47-8

110   John Kirvan, 50.

111   Ibid., 41-2.

112   Carl Sagan, *Pale Blue Dot: A Vision of the Human Future in Space* (New York: Penguin Random House, 1994).

113   Pirkei Avot, 2:16, as translated and interpreted by Rabbi Rami Shapiro in *Wisdom of the Jewish Sages: A Modern Reading of Pirke Avot* (New York City: Bell Tower, 1995).

Title from Hard Ball Press

A Great Vision: A Militant Family's Journey Through the Twentieth Century, Richard March

Caring: 1199 Nursing Home Workers Tell Their Story, Tim Sheard, ed.

Fight For Your Long Day, Classroom Edition, by Alex Kudera

Good Trouble: A Shoeleather History of Nonviolent Direct Action, Steve Thornton

I Just Got Elected, Now What? A New Union Officer's Handbook, 3rd Edtion, Bill Barry

I Still Can't Fly: Confessions of a Lifelong Troublemaker, Kevin John Carroll

In Hiding – A Thriller, Timothy Sheard

Justice Is Our Love In Action: Poetry & Art for the Resistance, Steward Acuff (author), Mitch Klein (Artist)

Legacy Costs: The Story of a Factory Town, Richard Hudelson

Love Dies – A Thriller, Timothy Sheard

The Man Who Fell From the Sky – Bill Fletcher, Jr.

Murder of a Post Office Manager – A Legal Thriller, Paul Felton

My Open Heart: 1199 Nursing Home Workers Tell Their Story

New York Hustle: Pool Rooms, School Rooms and Street Corner, A Memoir, Stan Maron

Sixteen Tons – A Novel, Kevin Corley

Throw Out the Water – Sequel to Sixteen Tons, Kevin Corley

The Union Member's Complete Guide, 2nd Edition, Updated & Revised, Michael Mauer

Union Made, Eric Lotke

Welcome to the Union (pamphlet), Michael Mauer

What Did You Learn at Work Today? The Forbidden Lessons of Labor Education, Helena Worthen

Winning Richmond: How a Progressive Alliance Won City Hall – Gayle McLaughlin

With Our Loving Hands: 1199 Nursing Home Workers Tell Their Story, Timothy Sheard, ed.

Woman Missing – A Mill Town Mystery, Linda Nordquist

The Lenny Moss Mysteries (in order of release) –
Timothy Sheard

This Won't Hurt A Bit

Some Cuts Never Heal

A Race Against Death

Slim To None

No Place To Be Sick

A Bitter Pill

Someone Has To Die

One Foot in the Grave

All Bleeding Stops Eventually